TRADE ISSUES, POLICIES

EUROPEAN UNION - U.S. TRADE AND INVESTMENT RELATIONS

TRADE ISSUES, POLICIES AND LAWS

Additional books in this series can be found on Nova's website at:

https://www.novapublishers.com/catalog/index.php?cPath=23_29&seriesp=
Trade+
Issues%2C+Policies+and+Laws

Additional e-books in this series can be found on Nova's website at:

https://www.novapublishers.com/catalog/index.php?cPath=23_29&seriespe=
Trade+
Issues%2C+Policies+and+Laws

TRADE ISSUES, POLICIES AND LAWS

EUROPEAN UNION - U.S. TRADE AND INVESTMENT RELATIONS

LINUS R. WILKENS
EDITOR

Nova Science Publishers, Inc.
New York

For permission to use material from this book please contact us:
Telephone 631-231-7269; Fax 631-231-8175
Web Site: http://www.novapublishers.com

NOTICE TO THE READER

The Publisher has taken reasonable care in the preparation of this book, but makes no expressed or implied warranty of any kind and assumes no responsibility for any errors or omissions. No liability is assumed for incidental or consequential damages in connection with or arising out of information contained in this book. The Publisher shall not be liable for any special, consequential, or exemplary damages resulting, in whole or in part, from the readers' use of, or reliance upon, this material. Any parts of this book based on government reports are so indicated and copyright is claimed for those parts to the extent applicable to compilations of such works.

Independent verification should be sought for any data, advice or recommendations contained in this book. In addition, no responsibility is assumed by the publisher for any injury and/or damage to persons or property arising from any methods, products, instructions, ideas or otherwise contained in this publication.

This publication is designed to provide accurate and authoritative information with regard to the subject matter covered herein. It is sold with the clear understanding that the Publisher is not engaged in rendering legal or any other professional services. If legal or any other expert assistance is required, the services of a competent person should be sought. FROM A DECLARATION OF PARTICIPANTS JOINTLY ADOPTED BY A COMMITTEE OF THE AMERICAN BAR ASSOCIATION AND A COMMITTEE OF PUBLISHERS.

LIBRARY OF CONGRESS CATALOGING-IN-PUBLICATION DATA

Available upon request

ISBN : 978-1-60741-886-3

Published by Nova Science Publishers, Inc. ✦ *New York*

CONTENTS

PREFACE

This book examines the United States and the 27-member European Union (EU), which share a huge, dynamic, and mutually beneficial economic partnership. Not only is the EU-U.S. commercial relationship, what many call the transatlantic economy, the largest in the world, it is also arguably the most important. Agreement between the two partners in the past has been critical to making the world and financial system more open and efficient. Given the high level of commercial interactions, trade tensions and disputes are not unexpected.

Chapter 1 - In May 2003, the United States, Canada, and Argentina initiated a dispute with the European Union concerning the EU's *de facto* moratorium on biotechnology product approvals, in place since 1998. Although the EU effectively lifted the moratorium in May 2004 by approving a genetically engineered (GE) corn variety (MON8 10), the three complainants pursued the case, in part because a number of EU member states continue to block already approved biotech products. Industry estimates are that the moratorium costs U.S. corn growers some $300 million in exports to the EU annually. U.S. officials also contend that the EU moratorium threatens U.S. agricultural exports to other parts of the world where the EU approach to regulating agricultural biotechnology is taking hold. On November 21, 2006, the WTO 's Dispute Settlement Body (DSB) adopted the dispute panel's report, which ruled that a moratorium had existed, that bans on EU-approved GE crops in six EU member countries violated WTO rules, and that the EU failed to ensure that its approval procedures were conducted without "undue delay." The EU has announced it will not appeal the ruling. The United States and EU agreed on November 21, 2007 (subsequently extended to January 11, 2008), as a deadline for EU implementation of the panel report. On January

11, the U.S. Trade Representative announced that, while it was reserving its rights to retaliate, it would hold off seeking a compliance ruling while the United State s sought to normalize trade in biotechnology products with the EU. In a related development, France, citing environmental concerns, announced a ban on cultivation of MON810. During the 111th Congress, Members with agricultural interests may debate the issue of whether to continue a dialogue with the EU on re-establishing trade in biotechnology products or to seek retaliation for presumed lack of EU compliance with the panel decision.

Chapter 2 - This chapter describes the European Union (EU), its evolution, governing institutions, trade policy, and efforts to forge common foreign and defense policies. The report also addresses the EU-U.S. and EU-NATO relationships, which may be of interest to the second session of the 110th Congress. For more information, see CRS Report RS21344, *European Union Enlargement*, by Kristin Archick, and CRS Report RL34381, *European Union-U.S. Trade and Investment Relations: Key Issues*, coordinated by Raymond Ahearn.

Chapter 3 - The United States and EU share a huge, dynamic, and mutually beneficial economic relationship. Not only are trade and investment ties between the two partners huge in absolute terms, but the EU share of U.S. global trade and investment flows has remained high and relatively constant over time, despite the rise of Asian trade and investment flows. These robust commercial ties provide consumers on both sides of the Atlantic with major benefits in terms of jobs and access to capital and new technologies.

Agreements between the two partners in the past have been critical to making the world trading system more open and efficient. At the same time, the commercial relationship is subject to a number of trade disputes and disagreements that potentially could have adverse political and economic repercussions.

Washington and Brussels currently are working to resolve a number of issues, including a dispute between the aerospace manufacturers, Airbus and Boeing, and conflicts over hormone-treated beef, bio-engineered food products, and protection of geographical indicators. The Airbus-Boeing dispute involves allegations of unfair subsidization while the other disputes are rooted in different U.S.-EU approaches to regulation, as well as social preferences. Simultaneously, the two sides have cooperated to liberalize the transatlantic air services market and are working on harmonizing and/or liberalizing financial markets. Competition agencies in the U.S. and EU are also moving towards substantial convergence in some areas of antitrust enforcement. A new institutional structure, the Transatlantic Economic Council (TEC), was established in 2007 to advance bilateral efforts to reduce regulatory and other barriers to trade.

Congress has taken a strong interest in many of these issues. By both proposing and passing legislation, Congress has supported the efforts of U.S. industrial and agricultural interests to gain better access to EU markets. Congress has pressured the executive branch to take a harder line against the EU in resolving some disputes, but has also cooperated with the Administration in crafting compromise solutions. Primarily through oversight in the second session of the 110th Congress, many Members of Congress can be expected to support efforts to resolve existing disputes and to maintain an equitable sharing of the costs and benefits of the commercial relationship with the EU.

This chapter starts with background information and data on the commercial relationship and then discusses selective issues associated with trade in agricultural products, trade in services, and foreign direct investment. A concluding section assesses prospects for future cooperation and conflict.

Chapter 4 - Soon after the Doha Round of multilateral trade negotiations came to a standstill in July 2006, the European Union (EU) announced its intention to enter into more bilateral and regional free trade agreements (FTAs). While the EU historically has been a leading force for preferential trade agreements, its main priority from 2001-2006 was negotiating an ambitious Doha Round agreement. Given that the EU is a global economic superpower, its resumption of a bilateral and preferential trade strategy has implications for the global trading system, as well as for U.S. trade interests. As articulated in an October 2006 report, the EU will prioritize FTAs with regions and countries according to their economic potential rather than on development aims. The July 2008 breakdown of the Doha negotiations may reinforce this approach. This chapter summarizes the EU's new initiative, casts the initiative in historical perspective, and assesses the implications of this shift for the global trading system and for U.S. interests. See also CRS Report RL30608, *EU-U.S. Economic Ties: Framework, Scope, and Magnitude,* by William H. Cooper.

Chapter 5 - The United States and the European Union (EU) economic relationship is the largest in the world—and it is growing. The modern U.S.-European economic relationship has evolved since World War II, broadening as the six-member European Community expanded into the present 27-member European Union. The ties have also become more complex and interdependent, covering a growing number and type of trade and financial activities.

In 2007, $1,602.1 billion flowed between the United States and the EU on the current account, the most comprehensive measure of U.S. trade flows. The EU as a unit is the largest merchandise trading partner of the United States. In 2007, the EU accounted for $247.3 billion of total U.S. exports (or 21.3%) and for $354.7 billion of total U.S. imports (or 18.2%) for a U.S. trade deficit of $107.4 billion. The EU is also the largest U.S. trade partner when trade in services is added to trade in merchandise, accounting for $182.5 billion (or 38.0% of the total in U.S. services exports) and $145.8 billion (or 42.7% of total U.S. services imports) in 2007. In addition, in 2007, a net $175.5 billion *flowed* from U.S. residents to EU countries into direct investments, while a net $148.4 billion *flowed* from EU residents to direct investments in the United States.

Policy disputes arise between the United States and the EU generating tensions which sometimes lead to bilateral trade disputes. Yet, in spite of these disputes, the U.S.-EU economic relationship remains dynamic. It is a relationship that is likely to grow in importance assuming the trends toward globalization and the enlargement of the EU continue, forcing more trade and investment barriers to fall. Economists indicate that an expanded relationship would bring economic benefits to both sides in the form of wider choices of goods and services and greater investment opportunities.

But increasing economic interdependence brings challenges as well as benefits. As the U.S. and EU economies continue to integrate, some sectors or firms will "lose out" to increased competition and will resist the forces of change. Greater economic integration also challenges long-held notions of "sovereignty," as national or regional policies have extraterritorial impact. Similarly, accepted understanding of "competition," "markets," and other economic concepts are tested as national borders dissolve with closer integration of economies.

U.S. and EU policymakers are likely to face the task of how to manage the increasingly complex bilateral economic relationship in ways that maximize benefits and keep frictions to a minimum, including developing new frameworks. For Members during the 111th Congress, it could mean weighing the benefits of greater economic integration against the costs to constituents in the context of overall U.S. national interests.

The bilateral economic relationship between the United States and the European Union (EU) is the largest such relationship in the world—and it is growing.[1] It is a relationship forged over several centuries, since the European colonization of North America.

The modern U.S.-European economic relationship has evolved since World War II. It has broadened as the six-member European Community expanded into the present 27-member European Union. The ties have also become more complex, covering a growing number and type of trade and financial activities that intertwine the economies on both sides of the Atlantic into an increasingly interdependent relationship. For Members of Congress and other policymakers, the EU remains a significant participant in the U.S. economy and a major factor in policy considerations. For example, the EU and its members are influential members of the World Trade Organization (WTO), the Organization for Economic Cooperation and Development (OECD), the International Monetary Fund (IMF) and the World Bank. These countries, together with the United States, play decisive roles in developing and implementing the missions of those institutions.

Despite the tightness of the bilateral relationship, policy tensions arise generating tensions within the relationship, sometimes leading to bilateral trade disputes.[2] The issues that arise are becoming more complex, reflecting the growing integration of the U.S. and EU economies. Yet, in spite of these disputes, the U.S.-EU economic relationship remains dynamic and one within which trillions of dollars of economic activity transpire.

This chapter provides background information and analysis of the U.S.-EU economic relationship for Members of the 111th Congress as they contemplate the costs and benefits of closer U.S. economic ties with the EU. It examines the economic and political framework of the relationship and the scope and magnitude of the ties based on data from various sources. In addition, the report analyzes the implications these factors have for U.S. economic policy toward the EU. The report will be revised as events warrant.

Chapter 6 - The United States and the European Union (EU) share a huge, dynamic, and mutually beneficial economic partnership. Not only is the U.S.-EU trade and investment relationship the largest in the world, but it is also arguably the most important. Agreement between the two partners in the past has been critical to making the world trading system more open and efficient.

Given the high level of U.S.-EU commercial interactions, trade tensions and disputes are not unexpected. In the past, U.S.-EU trade relations have witnessed periodic episodes of rising trade tensions and conflicts, only to be followed by successful efforts at dispute settlement. This ebb and flow of trade tensions occurred again in 2006 with high-profile disputes involving the Doha Round of multilateral trade negotiations and production subsidies for the commercial aircraft sector.

Major U.S.-EU trade disputes have varied causes. Some disputes stem from demands from producer interests for support or protection. Trade conflicts involving agriculture, aerospace, steel, and 'contingency protection' fit prominently into this grouping. These conflicts tend to be prompted by traditional trade barriers such as subsidies, tariffs, or industrial policy instruments, where the economic dimensions of the conflict predominate. Other conflicts arise when the U.S. or the EU initiate actions or measures to protect or promote their political and economic interests, often in the absence of significant private sector pressures. The underlying cause of these disputes over such issues as sanctions, unilateral trade actions, and preferential trade agreements are different foreign policy goals and priorities of Brussels and Washington. Still other conflicts stem from an array of domestic regulatory policies that reflect differing social and environmental values and objectives. Conflicts over hormone-treated beef, bio-engineered food products, protection of the audio-visual sector, and aircraft hushkits, for example, are rooted in different U.S.-EU regulatory approaches, as well as social preferences.

These three categories of trade conflicts — traditional, foreign policy, and regulatory — possess varied potential for future trade conflict. This is due mostly to the fact that bilateral and multilateral agreements governing the settlement of disputes affect each category of disputes differently. By providing a fairly detailed map of permissible actions and obligations, trade agreements can dampen the inclination of governments to supply protection and private sector parties to demand protection.

In sum, U.S.-EU bilateral trade conflicts do not appear to be as ominous and threatening as the media often portray, but they are not ephemeral distractions either. Rather they appear to have real, albeit limited, economic and political consequences for the bilateral relationship. From an economic perspective, the disputes may also be weakening efforts of the two partners to provide strong leadership to the global trading system.

In: European Union - U.S. Trade and Investment... ISBN: 978-1-60741-886-3
Editors: Linus R. Wilkens pp.1-9 © 2010 Nova Science Publishers, Inc.

Chapter 1

AGRICULTURAL BIOTECHNOLOGY: THE U.S.-EU DISPUTE

Charles E. Hanrahan

SUMMARY

In May 2003, the United States, Canada, and Argentina initiated a dispute with the European Union concerning the EU's *de facto* moratorium on biotechnology product approvals, in place since 1998. Although the EU effectively lifted the moratorium in May 2004 by approving a genetically engineered (GE) corn variety (MON8 10), the three complainants pursued the case, in part because a number of EU member states continue to block already approved biotech products. Industry estimates are that the moratorium costs U.S. corn growers some $300 million in exports to the EU annually. U.S. officials also contend that the EU moratorium threatens U.S. agricultural exports to other parts of the world where the EU approach to regulating agricultural biotechnology is taking hold. On November 21, 2006, the WTO 's Dispute Settlement Body (DSB) adopted the dispute panel's report, which ruled that a moratorium had existed, that bans on EU-approved GE crops in six EU member countries violated WTO rules, and that the EU failed to ensure that its approval procedures were conducted without "undue delay." The EU has announced it will not appeal the ruling. The United States and EU agreed on November 21, 2007 (subsequently extended to January 11, 2008), as a deadline for EU implementation of the panel report. On January 11, the U.S. Trade Representative announced that, while it was reserving its rights to retaliate, it would hold off seeking a compliance ruling while the United State s sought to normalize trade in biotechnology products with the EU. In a related development, France, citing environmental concerns, announced a ban on cultivation of MON810. During the 111th Congress, Members with agricultural interests may debate the issue of whether to continue a dialogue with the EU on re-establishing trade in biotechnology products or to seek retaliation for presumed lack of EU compliance with the panel decision.

THE DISPUTE PANEL' RULING

The WTO dispute panel found that the EU had maintained a moratorium on approvals of genetically engineered crops between June 1999 and the beginning of panel deliberations in August 2003.[1] The EU had claimed that there were no measures imposing a moratorium. The panel agreed with the United States and the co-complainants that marketing or import prohibitions on GE products in six EU countries (Austria, France, Germany, Greece, Italy, and Luxembourg) violated the WTO's Agreement on Sanitary and Phytosanitary (SPS) Measures, which requires such measures to be based on science and risk assessment. The panel upheld the complainants' charge that the EU also violated the SPS agreement by not ensuring that approvals for 24 of 27 genetically modified (GM) products in the approval pipeline were carried out without "undue delay."

The dispute panel's ruling dismissed several other U.S. and co-complainant claims, including claims that EU approval procedures were not based on appropriate risk assessment; that the EU unfairly applied different risk assessment standards for GE processing agents; and that the EU had unjustifiably discriminated between WTO members. The panel made no recommendations as to how the EU should bring its practices in line with WTO rules, nor did the ruling require the EU to change its regulatory framework for approving GE products. The EU announced on December 19, 2006, that it would not appeal the panel's ruling in the case. The United States and EU agreed that a reasonable period of time would be until November 21, 2007, a deadline subsequently extended by mutual agreement until January 11, 2008. Time would likely be required to reach intra-EU agreement to lift the prohibitions on already approved GE products or to launch court challenges to require member countries to lift their prohibitions on GE products.[2]

BACKGROUND

In May 2003, the United States, Canada, and Argentina requested consultations, the first step in WTO dispute settlement, with the EU concerning the latter's *de facto* moratorium (since 1998) on approving new GE products. U.S. agricultural interests contended that these policies not only blocked their exports to the EU, but also fueled unwarranted concerns about the safety of agricultural biotechnology throughout the world. Although the EU recommenced approvals in May 2004 with the approval of a GE corn variety for human consumption, a number of EU member states continue to block dissemination of approved biotech varieties. The EU restarted its approval process following adoption of new labeling and traceability rules for GE crops and foods in 2003.[3]

The United States accounted for 50% of the 282 million acres (114.3 million hectares) planted globally with GE crops in 2007.[4] In 2008, 92% of all U.S. soybean, 86% of U.S. cotton, and 80% of U.S. corn acres were planted with GE varieties, designed mainly to control pests (weeds and insects).[5] GE production is not segregated from production from conventional varieties because the U.S. regulatory system recognizes GE crops (once approved for commercialization) as substantially equivalent to non-GE varieties. Gaining market acceptance of GE crops within the United States has been easier than overseas, however, where, in markets like the EU, consumers and their governments have been more wary of biotechnology.

With minor exceptions, the EU and its member states approved no GE products between 1998 and 2004. As of January 2004, 22 GE products or crops were awaiting approval. A bloc of EU states had effectively halted the release of any new GE crops into the environment, saying that they would not implement the EU-wide legislation for approvals until new, stricter regulations for labeling and tracing GE-containing products (discussed below) took effect.[6]

In the three years before the *de facto* ban, U.S. corn exports to the EU averaged about $300 million annually, according to USDA data (Spain and Portugal were the largest EU importers). During the ban, they declined to less than one-tenth of that value annually—the result, according to analysts, of the

EU's moratorium on the approval of new corn varieties already approved in the United States. Although one variety of biotech corn was approved by the EU prior to the moratorium, the United States grew other varieties. Thus, U.S. export of any corn to the EU was impractical because of the difficulty of segregating approved from unapproved varieties.

THE WTO CASE

The United States and co-complainants argued that the EU moratorium violated the WTO Agreement on the Application of Sanitary and Phytosanitary (SPS) Measures. The SPS agreement permits countries to regulate crops and food products to protect health and the environment, but their rules must be scientifically justified, and approval procedures must occur without undue delay. U.S. interests contend that there is no scientific evidence that GE food and feed crops are substantially different from, or any less safe than, conventional varieties, a conclusion they say even European scientific authorities have reached. The United States contends that EU biotechnology measures also are inconsistent with provisions of other WTO agreements, namely the Technical Barriers to Trade Agreement (TBT), the General Agreement on Tariffs and Trade (GATT), and the Agreement on Agriculture.

EU officials counter that their cautious approach to regulating biotechnology is necessary to cultivate trust among European consumers. At the same time, they also assert that they have shown good faith in moving quickly to restart the approval process. In May 2004, the EU effectively ended the moratorium by approving a GE corn variety (Syngenta Bt- 11) for human consumption. Since then, the EU has approved GE corn varieties (Monsanto's NK603) for both human and animal consumption, Pioneer's 1570 corn for feed use, and 17 strains of GE corn seed (all derived from the MON 810 strain approved in 1998) for commercial use.

DIFFERING REGULATORY APPROACHES

The United States has embraced the concept of substantial equivalence with regard to GE products: if a GE product is substantially the same as its conventional counterpart, it should be regulated no differently than the conventional product. The EU, on the other hand, takes a "precautionary approach," which means that if scientific evidence is insufficient or inconclusive regarding a practice's or product's potential dangers to human or environmental health, it should be more vigorously regulated or even prohibited if there are reasonable grounds for concern, thus providing a safeguard against future unforeseen problems. Under this approach, the products of biotechnology are deemed to be inherently different from their conventional counterparts and to require a separate regulatory regime.

United States

The basic federal guidance for regulating biotechnology products is the *Coordinated Framework for Regulation ofBiotechnology*.[7] One of its key principles is that GE products should be regulated according to their characteristics and unique features—not according to their method of production. Once approved, food products do not have to be labeled as to whether or not they contain any genetically modified organisms, except to the extent that a GE food is substantially different (e.g., contains an allergen or has a changed nutritional content). Because they are deemed substantially equivalent, GE products are regulated under existing federal statutory authorities.[8]

European Union

The EU has established separate structures specifically for approving GE products and for labeling products derived from them. Currently, the key measure is Council Directive 2001/18 (as amended in July 2003) which spells out steps for assessing human health and environmental risks before any GE product can be released into the environment or marketed.[9] Prior to the 2003 amendments, the competent authority in the EU member state where the product was to be released was responsible for assessing its safety and, if approved, notifying other member states, opening the way for marketing throughout the EU (with EU-level intervention if one member state disagreed with another's decision). The amended directive provides for a "one-door-one-key" approach, whereby the European Food Safety Authority (EFSA) conducts all scientific risk assessments and communicates risks to the public. Then, the EU Council of Ministers decides whether or not to approve a GE product for the EU market. EU regulations empower the European Commission to approve applications by default if the Council of Ministers fails to act on them within three months.

LABELING AND TRACEABILITY

The WTO case does not involve new, stricter EU labeling and traceability regulations, which, U.S. agricultural interests argue, continued to discriminate against U.S. exports even after the GE product approval moratorium was lifted. The labeling and traceability regulations, adopted in July 2003, require that most foods, ingredients, and (for the first time) animal feeds from GE products be labeled, even if they no longer contain detectable traces. The regulations (1830/2003 on the Traceability and Labeling of GMOs and 1829/2003 on Genetically Modified (GM) Food and Feed) were implemented in April 2004.

Under the regulations, a tolerance level for non-GE foods, feeds, and processed products of 0.9% is set for allowable "adventitious presence" (AP)—that is, unintended, low-level presence—of an EU-approved GE substance. All products with more than 0.9% must be labeled as containing GE products. Products like meat, milk, and eggs from animals fed or treated with GE materials will not have to be labeled, however. Traceability provisions now require all firms that produce, store, move, or process GE products to track and keep records on them from farm to consumer. Compliance with the EU labeling rule requires segregation of GE crops and foods derived from them from the time they are planted all the way through the processing and marketing chain. This entails prevention of pollen drift from GE to non-GE fields; and difficult and costly handling procedures such as using separate equipment, storage, and shipping containers, or at least painstakingly cleaning them. U.S. interests argue that food companies forced to label accurately all GE products face huge risks and liabilities. All of these problems discriminate against U.S. shipments—even though they are as safe as "conventional" shipments, they contend. In practice, many U.S. manufacturers have opted not to market GE products in the EU, in part due to the EU's stricter GE regulations.[10]

The European Commission is currently discussing new technical guidelines for the allowable level of genetically engineered organisms in food and feed shipments for GE products that have been approved in exporting countries but not the EU.

DIFFERING PUBLIC ATTITUDES?

Differing U.S. and EU perspectives may reflect the fact that U.S. consumers apparently have been not only less fearful of GE foods than their European counterparts, but also more confident in their food safety regulators. According to USDA's Economic Research Service (ERS), surveys of consumer attitudes toward GE products, conducted both here and overseas, have yielded mixed results. Still, "U.S. consumers have voiced little objection to genetically modified foods, while EU consumers have been vocal in their disapproval," ERS observed.[11]

Europeans may be much more wary of changes in how their food is produced due to a series of recent food safety crises during the 1990s. Bovine spongiform encephalopathy (BSE, or "mad cow disease") emerged in the United Kingdom and spread to other parts of Europe. U.K. food safety authorities first insisted that the disease could not be transmitted to humans eating meat from BSE-infected animals. By 1996 scientific evidence indicated there was a link between some cases of a similar human disease and consumption of BSE-contaminated beef. In 1999, high levels of dioxin were found in meat products and eggs originating in Belgium. Also, foot-and-mouth disease (FMD) outbreaks in Europe added to consumer concerns and to their "waning faith in regulatory agencies," according to the Pew Charitable Trust's Initiative on Food and Biotechnology. Pew is careful to point out that these crises have not been caused by GE food, but that GE food has been caught up in the general suspicion about food safety. Environmental groups in the EU, such as Greenpeace and Friends of the Earth, also have raised concerns about environmental impacts.

Recently, concerns have been voiced by European grain and feedstuffs traders and compound feed manufacturers about EU regulations and attitudes about GE corn and soybeans.[12] They point to short supplies and high prices for feedstuffs and call for changes in the EU regulations that impose strict limits on adventitious presence and that have helped create a shortage of feed supplies in the EU. COCERAL, the association of EU feedstuffs traders, has pointed out that neither Argentina nor Brazil, who along with the United States supply the bulk of annual EU feed supplies, could guarantee that its corn and soybean shipments contain only EU-approved GMOs.

CONGRESSIONAL INTEREST

In the last Congress, Members representing agricultural interests urged the United States to take an aggressive stance with respect to EU biotechnology regulations. Senator Grassley, the Ranking Member of the Senate Finance Committee, expressed hope that the EU would soon come into compliance with the WTO ruling in the biotechnology case. He noted that, although he would have preferred the U.S. Trade Representative to take a harder line in the case, he recognized that a "hard approach" of seeking retaliation might not be successful.[13] At the same time, many lawmakers are well aware of the risks involved in escalating U.S.-EU trade tensions to new heights.

How to proceed with the EU on biotechnology trade is an issue that the Bush Administration left unresolved. The options for the Obama Administration appear to be either to continue a dialogue with the EU on biotechnology policy and trade or to pursue retaliation for failure to comply with the earlier adverse ruling. Before the United States could impose retaliatory measures, however, it would have to request establishment of a panel to determine whether the EU had complied with the November 21, 2006, decision in the dispute. As the 111th Congress monitors the Administration's conduct of agricultural trade policy, the issues raised by the U.S.-EU biotechnology dispute will likely remain on the agenda.

End Notes

[1] Background on the U.S.-EU biotechnology dispute is available at
   http://www.wto.org/english/tratop_e/dispu_e/ cases_e/ds291_e.htm.
[2] See "EU Council Rejects Proposals to Lift Bans on GMO Products" *in Inside U.S. Trade*,
   December 22, 2006, at
   http://www.insidetrade.com/secure/dsply_nl_txt.asp?f=wto2002.ask&dh=70507021&q=
   gmo.
[3] The EU's labeling and traceability regulation is at http://europa.eu.int/eur-
   lex/pri/en/oj/dat/2003/l_268/ l_26820031018en00240028.pdf.
[4] Data are from ISAAA Brief 37-2007, *Global Status of Commercialized Biotech/GM Crops:
   2007*, at http://www.isaaa.org.
[5] USDA, Economic Research Service website, *Adoption of Genetically Engineered Crops in the
   U.S.*, at http://www.ers.usda.gov/data/BiotechCrops/.

[6] Before the moratorium, the EU had approved the commercial release of 18 genetically modified organisms (GMOs), including MON810 and "Roundup-Ready" soybeans.

[7] Executive Office of the President, Office of Science and Technology Policy (51 FR 23302), *Coordinated Framework for Regulation of Biotechnology*, June 26, 1986, viewed at http://usbiotechreg.nbii.gov/
CoordinatedFrameworkForRegulationOfBiotechnology1986.pdf.

[8] See http://heinonline.org/HOL/Page?handle=hein.fedreg/051123&id=96&collection=fedreg.

[9] See the EU's *Directive on the release of genetically modified organisms*, together with amending acts, at http://europa.eu/scadplus/leg/en/lvb/l28130.htm.

[10] Personal communication with Economic Research Service, January 21, 2005.

[11] Details on these surveys can be found at ERS, *Economic Issues in Agricultural Biotechnology* (Information Bulletin No. 762), February 2001, pp. 28-30. In December 2006, the Pew Initiative on Food and Biotechnology released a new survey of U.S. attitudes on GM foods which, Pew said, determined that Americans' knowledge of them remains low, that their opposition to such foods has softened somewhat since 2001 (from 58% to 48%), and support remains stable at 27%. Survey results can be found at http://pewagbiotech.org/research/2006update/2.php.

[12] "GMO zero tolerance devastating for EU feed industry," from *AgBioWorld*, July 19, 2007, viewed at
http://www.agbioworld.org/newsletter_wm/index.php?caseid=archive&newsid=2747.

[13] "U.S. To Hold Off on GMO Retaliation Against EU, France Bans GMO Corn", *Inside U.S. Trade*, January 18, 2008, viewed at
http://www.insidetrade.com/secure/dsply_nl_txt.asp?f=wto2002.ask&dh=107026683&q=.

In: European Union - U.S. Trade and Investment… ISBN: 978-1-60741-886-3
Editors: Linus R. Wilkens pp.11-20   © 2010 Nova Science Publishers, Inc.

Chapter 2

THE EUROPEAN UNION: QUESTIONS AND ANSWERS

Kristin Archick

SUMMARY

This chapter describes the European Union (EU), its evolution, governing institutions, trade policy, and efforts to forge common foreign and defense policies. The chapter also addresses the EU-U.S. and EU-NATO relationships, which may be of interest to the second session of the 110th Congress.

WHAT IS THE EU?

The EU is a treaty-based, institutional framework that defines and manages economic and political cooperation among its 27 member states (Austria, Belgium, Bulgaria, Cyprus, the Czech Republic, Denmark, Estonia, Finland, France, Germany, Greece, Hungary, Ireland, Italy, Latvia, Lithuania, Luxembourg, Malta, the Netherlands, Poland, Portugal, Romania, Slovakia, Slovenia, Spain, Sweden, and the United Kingdom). The Union is the latest stage in a process of European integration begun after World War II to promote peace and economic prosperity in Europe. Its founders hoped that by creating communities of shared sovereignty — initially in areas of coal and steel production, trade, and nuclear energy — another war in Europe would be unthinkable. Since the 1950s, this European integration project has expanded to encompass other economic sectors, a customs union, a single market in which goods, people, and capital move freely, a common agricultural policy, and a common currency (the euro). Over the last decade, EU member states have taken significant steps toward political integration as well, with decisions to develop a common foreign policy and closer police and judicial cooperation.

How Does the EU Work?

The EU represents a unique form of cooperation among sovereign states; it has been built through a series of binding treaties. EU members work together through common institutions (see next question). The EU is divided into three "pillars;" subjects and decision-making processes differ in each. Pillar One is the European Community, which encompasses economic, trade, and social policies ranging from agriculture to education. In Pillar One areas, by far the most developed and far-reaching, members have largely pooled their national sovereignty and work together in EU institutions to set policy and promote their collective interests. Decisions in Pillar One often have a supranational character because most are made by a majority voting system. Pillar Two aims to establish a Common Foreign and Security Policy (CFSP) to permit joint action in foreign and security affairs. Pillar Three seeks to create a Justice and Home Affairs (JHA) policy to foster common internal security measures and closer police and judicial coordination. Under Pillars Two and Three, members have agreed to cooperate but decision-making is intergovernmental and by consensus. Thus, members retain more discretion and the right to veto certain measures.

How Is the EU Governed?

The EU is governed by several institutions. They do not correspond exactly to the traditional division of power in democratic governments. Rather, they embody the EU's dual supranational and intergovernmental character:

- The *European Commission* is essentially the EU's executive and has the sole right of legislative initiative. It upholds the interests of the Union as a whole and ensures that the provisions of the EU treaties are carried out properly. The 27 Commissioners are appointed by the member states for five-year terms. Each Commissioner holds a distinct portfolio (e.g., agriculture). The Commission represents the EU internationally and negotiates with third countries primarily in areas falling under Pillar One. However, the Commission is primarily an administrative entity that serves the Council of Ministers.
- The *Council of the European Union* (*Council of Ministers*) is comprised of ministers from the national governments. As the main decision- making body, the Council enacts legislation based on proposals put forward by the Commission. Different ministers participate depending on the subject under consideration (e.g., economics ministers could convene to discuss unemployment policy). Most decisions are made by majority vote, but some areas — such as CFSP and taxation — require unanimity. The Presidency of the Council rotates among the member states for a period of six months.
- The *European Council* brings together the Heads of State or Government of the member states and the Commission President at least twice a year. It acts principally as a strategic guide and driving force for EU policy.
- The *European Parliament* consists of 785 members. Since 1979, they have been directly elected in each member state for five-year terms under a system of proportional representation based on population. The Parliament cannot initiate legislation like national parliaments, but it shares "co-decision" power with the Council of Ministers in a number of areas, and can amend or reject the EU's budget.
- The *Court of Justice* interprets EU law and its rulings are binding; a *Court of Auditors* monitors the EU's financial management. A number of *advisory bodies* represent economic, social, and regional interests.

WHY AND HOW IS THE EU ENLARGING?

The EU sees enlargement as crucial to promoting stability and prosperity in Europe, and furthering the peaceful integration of the continent. The EU began as the European Coal and Steel Community in 1952 with six members (Belgium, France, Germany, Italy, Luxembourg, and the Netherlands). Denmark, Ireland, and the UK joined in 1973, Greece in 1981, Spain and Portugal in 1986, and Austria, Finland, and Sweden in 1995. With the end of the Cold War, the EU saw an historic opportunity to extend the political and economic benefits of membership to central and eastern Europe. On May 1, 2004, the EU welcomed 10 states (Cyprus, the Czech Republic, Estonia, Hungary, Latvia, Lithuania, Malta, Poland, Slovakia, and Slovenia) as new members. Bulgaria and Romania completed accession talks in December 2004 and acceded to the Union on January 1, 2007. Accession negotiations establish the terms under which applicants will meet and enforce EU rules and regulations. Turkey was recognized as an EU candidate in 1999 but remained in a separate category for several years as it sought to comply with the EU's political and economic criteria for membership. In October 2005, the EU opened accession talks with Turkey, but these are expected to take at least a decade to complete and have already encountered some difficulties. The EU has cautioned that the negotiations with Turkey are an "open-ended process, the outcome of which cannot be guaranteed." The EU also began accession talks with Croatia in October 2005. Macedonia was named as an EU candidate in December 2005, but no date has yet been set for the start of its membership talks.

WHAT WAS THE EU CONSTITUTION AND WHY A NEW REFORM TREATY?

In June 2004, the EU concluded work on a constitutional treaty that contained changes to the EU's governing institutions and decision-making processes. Commonly referred to as the "constitution," this new treaty grew out of previous EU efforts to institute internal reforms to enable an enlarged EU to function more effectively. The constitution also sought to boost the EU's visibility on the world stage. In order to come into effect, the constitution had to be ratified by all member states through either parliamentary approval or public referendum. The constitution's future was thrown into doubt following its rejection by French and Dutch voters in separate referendums in the spring of 2005. Reasons for its rejection varied, ranging from public unease with further EU enlargement to fears that it could lead to the creation of a European "superstate."

In December 2007, EU leaders approved a new reform treaty — the Lisbon Treaty — to essentially replace the proposed constitution. Although the term "constitution" was dropped, experts say that the Lisbon Treaty preserves over 90% of the substance of the original constitution. Major innovations include appointing a single individual to serve as president of the European Council, creating a new chief EU diplomat position, and simplifying EU voting procedures. EU officials presented the Lisbon Treaty as a document that could be ratified by parliaments, thereby avoiding risky public referendums in most EU states, except Ireland, which was required by law to hold a public vote. In June 2008, Irish voters rejected the Lisbon Treaty. Irish opponents argued that it would reduce Ireland's influence in the EU, undermine Ireland's neutrality, and eliminate its ability to set its own tax rates. EU leaders have called on the ratification process to continue in other EU states, and have given Irish officials until October 2008 to propose a way forward. EU officials hope that the Lisbon Treaty will still be able to enter into force before the next European Parliament elections in the spring of 2009.

DOES THE EU HAVE A FOREIGN POLICY?

The EU is seeking to build a Common Foreign and Security Policy (CFSP). Past attempts to further EU political integration foundered on national sovereignty concerns and different foreign policy prerogatives. But in 1993, EU members concluded that the Union must increase its weight in world affairs to match its growing economic clout. CFSP decision-making is dominated by member states; they develop common policies in areas in which they can reach consensus, and ensure that national policies are in line with agreed EU strategies and positions (e.g., imposing sanctions on Serbia). In 1997, EU leaders proposed creating a High Representative for CFSP; in 1999, they appointed Javier Solana, NATO's former Secretary General, to the position, which is often referred to as "Mr. CFSP". Many analysts credit Solana with boosting the EU's visibility on the world stage, and with forging EU consensus on issues such as the Balkans and the Middle East peace process. Skeptics argue, however, that the EU is still far from speaking with one voice on other key foreign policy challenges. The European Commission also plays a role internationally, but should not be confused with CFSP or its High Representative. Benita Ferrero-Waldner, the External Relations Commissioner, coordinates the Commission's diplomatic activities and manages its aid to non-member states. The Lisbon Treaty, if approved, would combine the Ferrero-Waldner and Solana posts into a single position.

DOES THE EU HAVE A DEFENSE POLICY?

The EU is also attempting to forge a European Security and Defense Policy (ESDP) to give CFSP a military backbone. Momentum for this project picked up speed in 1998, when former UK Prime Minister Tony Blair reversed Britain's traditional opposition to a European defense identity outside NATO; it intensified after NATO's 1999 Kosovo air campaign exposed serious European military deficiencies. In December 1999, the EU decided to establish an institutional decision-making framework for ESDP and a 60,000- strong rapid reaction force by 2003 — able to deploy within 60 days for at least a year — to undertake the "Petersberg tasks" (humanitarian assistance, search and rescue, peacekeeping, and peace enforcement). In June 2004, the EU agreed to enhance ESDP through the creation of several "battlegroups" of 1,500 troops each that will be able to reach trouble spots, especially in Africa, within 15 days. EU forces will not form a standing "EU army"; troops and assets at appropriate readiness levels will be drawn from existing national forces in the event of an EU operation. The EU has created three defense decision-making bodies, but improving military capabilities has been difficult, especially given flat or declining European defense budgets. Serious capability gaps exist in strategic airlift, command and control systems, intelligence, and other force multipliers.

WHAT IS THE RELATIONSHIP BETWEEN NATO AND THE EU?

The EU asserts that ESDP is intended to allow the EU to make decisions and conduct military operations "where NATO as a whole is not engaged;" ESDP is not aimed at usurping NATO's collective defense role. Most EU NATO members, led by the UK, insist that EU efforts to forge a defense arm be tied to NATO, as do U.S. policymakers. Advocates argue that building more robust European military capabilities for ESDP will also benefit the alliance. The NATO-EU relationship was formalized in December 2002, which paved the way for the implementation in March 2003 of "Berlin Plus," an arrangement permitting the EU "assured access" to NATO operational planning capabilities and "presumed access" to NATO common assets. "Berlin Plus" was designed to help ensure close NATO-EU links, and prevent a wasteful duplication of resources. Since then, the EU has launched several crisis management missions in the Balkans, Africa, and elsewhere, with varying degrees of NATO support. Nevertheless, NATO-EU relations remain somewhat strained. This is due in part to the differences in membership in both organizations and disputes between Turkey (a NATO member) and the EU. U.S. officials have also been wary that some EU member states, traditionally led by France, would like to build a more independent EU defense arm. New French President Nicolas Sarkozy, however, has taken a more pragmatic approach; he backs a strong ESDP, but has downplayed it as an alternative to NATO and supports closer NATO-EU cooperation.

DOES THE EU HAVE A TRADE POLICY?

Yes. EU member states have a common external trade policy in which the European Commission negotiates trade deals with other countries and trading blocs on behalf of the Union as a whole. The EU's trade policy is one of its most well-developed and integrated policies. It evolved along with the common market, which provides for the free movement of goods within the EU, to prevent one member state from importing foreign goods at cheaper prices due to lower tariffs and then re-exporting the items to another member with higher tariffs. The scope of the common trade policy has been extended to include negotiations on services and intellectual property in some cases. The Council of Ministers has the power to establish objectives for trade negotiations and can approve or reject agreements reached by the Commission. EU rules allow the Council to make trade decisions with a weighted voting system, but in practice, the Council tends to employ consensus. The Commission and the Council work together to set the common customs tariff, guide export policy, and decide on trade protection or retaliation measures where necessary. The EU also plays a leading role in the World Trade Organization (WTO).

HOW ARE U.S.-EU TRADE RELATIONS DOING?

The United States and the EU share the largest trade and investment relationship in the world. The value of two-way flows of goods, services, and income receipts from investment totaled $1.3 trillion in 2006. U.S. and European companies are also the biggest investors in each other's markets; total stock of two-way direct investment reached $2.2 trillion in 2006. Most of this economic relationship is harmonious, but trade tensions persist. One key dispute relates to government subsidies that the United States and EU allegedly provide to their respective civil aircraft manufacturers, Boeing and Airbus. In 2005, U.S.-EU talks to diffuse confrontation over this issue failed, and both sides have revived their complaints in the World Trade Organization (WTO). U.S.-EU conflicts over hormone-treated beef and bio-engineered food products also remain. Many analysts note that resolving U.S.-EU trade disputes has become increasingly difficult, perhaps partly because both sides are of roughly equal economic strength and neither has the ability to impose concessions on the other. Another factor may be that many disputes involve clashes in different domestic values, political priorities, and regulatory systems.

DOES THE UNITED STATES HAVE A FORMAL RELATIONSHIP WITH THE EU?

Yes. For decades, the United States and the EU (and its progenitors) have maintained diplomatic and economic ties. Washington has strongly supported European integration, and U.S. -EU trade and investment relations are extensive. The 1990 U.S. -EU Transatlantic Declaration set out principles for greater consultation, and established regular summit and ministerial meetings. In 1995, the New Transatlantic Agenda (NTA) and the EU-U.S. Joint Action Plan provided a framework for promoting stability and democracy together, responding to global changes, and expanding world trade. The NTA also sought to strengthen individual ties across the Atlantic, and launched a number of dialogues, including ones for business leaders and legislators.

WHO ARE U.S. OFFICIALS' COUNTERPARTS IN THE EU?

At least once a year, the U.S. president meets with the president of the European Commission and the EU's rotating presidency, represented by the head of government whose country holds it at the time of the meeting. For example, at the last U.S.-EU summit in June 2008, President Bush met with Commission President José Manuel Barroso and Prime Minister Janez Jansa of Slovenia, the presidency country during the first half of 2008. The U.S. Secretary of State's most frequent interlocutors are the High Representative for CFSP, the External Relations Commissioner, and the foreign minister of the EU presidency country. The U.S. Trade Representative's key interlocutor is the European Commissioner for Trade, who directs the EU's common external trade policy. Other U.S. cabinet-level officials interact with Commission counterparts or member state ministers in Council formation as issues arise. Numerous working-level relationships between U.S. and EU officials also exist. A Delegation in Washington, DC represents the European Commission in its dealings with the U.S. government, while the U.S. Mission to the European Union represents Washington's interests in Brussels.

HOW DO EUROPEAN COUNTRIES VIEW THE EU?

All EU member states believe that the Union magnifies their political and economic clout (i.e., the sum is greater than the parts). Nevertheless, the EU has always been divided between those members that seek an "ever closer union" through greater integration and those that prefer to keep the Union on an intergovernmental footing. For example, the UK has more frequently sought to guard its national sovereignty and, along with Denmark and Sweden, does not participate in the single European currency (the euro). Another classic divide in the EU falls along big versus small state lines. Small states are often cautious of initiatives that they fear could allow EU heavyweights to dominate the Union. Another key difference relates to security postures; Austria, Finland, Ireland, and Sweden practice non-aligned foreign and defense policies, which sometimes complicates the formulation of common European positions in these areas. In addition, the recent rounds of EU enlargement to the east have brought in many new members with histories of Soviet domination, which often color their views on issues ranging from EU reform to relations with Russia; at times, such differences have caused frictions with older EU member states and have slowed EU decision making.

In: European Union - U.S. Trade and Investment... ISBN: 978-1-60741-886-3
Editors: Linus R. Wilkens pp.21-62   © 2010 Nova Science Publishers, Inc.

Chapter 3

EUROPEAN UNION - U.S. TRADE AND INVESTMENT RELATIONS: KEY ISSUES

Raymond J. Ahearn, John W. Fischer,
Charles B. Goldfarb, Charles E. Hanrahan,
Walter W. Eubanks and Janice E. Rubin

SUMMARY

The United States and EU share a huge, dynamic, and mutually beneficial economic relationship. Not only are trade and investment ties between the two partners huge in absolute terms, but the EU share of U.S. global trade and investment flows has remained high and relatively constant over time, despite the rise of Asian trade and investment flows. These robust commercial ties provide consumers on both sides of the Atlantic with major benefits in terms of jobs and access to capital and new technologies.

Agreements between the two partners in the past have been critical to making the world trading system more open and efficient. At the same time, the commercial relationship is subject to a number of trade disputes and disagreements that potentially could have adverse political and economic repercussions.

Washington and Brussels currently are working to resolve a number of issues, including a dispute between the aerospace manufacturers, Airbus and Boeing, and conflicts over hormone-treated beef, bio-engineered food products, and protection of geographical indicators. The Airbus-Boeing dispute involves allegations of unfair subsidization while the other disputes are rooted in different U.S.-EU approaches to regulation, as well as social preferences. Simultaneously, the two sides have cooperated to liberalize the transatlantic air services market and are working on harmonizing and/or liberalizing financial markets. Competition agencies in the U.S. and EU are also moving towards substantial convergence in some areas of antitrust enforcement. A new institutional structure, the Transatlantic Economic Council (TEC), was established in 2007 to advance bilateral efforts to reduce regulatory and other barriers to trade.

Congress has taken a strong interest in many of these issues. By both proposing and passing legislation, Congress has supported the efforts of U.S. industrial and agricultural interests to gain better access to EU markets. Congress has pressured the executive branch to take a harder line against the EU in resolving some disputes, but has also cooperated with the Administration in crafting compromise solutions. Primarily through oversight in the second session of the 110th Congress, many Members of Congress can be expected to support efforts to resolve existing disputes and to maintain an equitable sharing of the costs and benefits of the commercial relationship with the EU.

This chapter starts with background information and data on the commercial relationship and then discusses selective issues associated with trade in agricultural products, trade in services, and foreign direct investment. A concluding section assesses prospects for future cooperation and conflict.

INTRODUCTION[1]

The United States and EU share the largest commercial relationship in the world. Not only are trade and investment ties between the two partners huge in absolute terms, but the EU share of U.S. global trade and investment flows has remained high and relatively constant over time, despite the rise of Asian trade and investment flows. These robust U.S.- EU commercial ties are mutually beneficial and provide consumers on both sides of the Atlantic with major benefits in terms of jobs and access to capital and new technologies.

Given the high level of commercial interactions, trade tensions and disputes are not unexpected. In the past, U.S.-EU trade relations have experienced periodic episodes of rising trade tensions and conflicts, only to be followed by successful efforts at dispute settlement. Policymakers and many academics tend to maintain that the U.S. and EU always have more in common than in dispute, and like to point out that trade disputes usually affect a small fraction (often estimated at 1-2 percent) of the trade in goods and services.

Currently, Washington and Brussels are working to resolve a number of issues, including a dispute between the aerospace manufacturers, Airbus and Boeing, and conflicts over hormone-treated beef, bio-engineered food products, and protection of geographical indicators. The Airbus-Boeing dispute involves allegations of unfair subsidization while the other disputes are rooted in different U.S.-EU approaches to regulation, as well as social preferences. Simultaneously, the two sides have cooperated to liberalize the transatlantic air services market and are working to harmonize and/or liberalize financial markets. Agencies in the U.S. and EU are also moving towards substantial convergence in some areas of antitrust enforcement. A new institutional structure, the Transatlantic Economic Council (TEC), was established in 2007 to advance bilateral efforts to reduce regulatory and other barriers to trade.

Congress has taken a strong interest in many of these issues. By both proposing and passing legislation, Congress has supported the efforts of U.S. industrial and agricultural interests to gain better access to EU markets. Congress has pressured the executive branch to take a harder line against the EU in resolving some disputes, but has also cooperated with the Administration in crafting compromise solutions.

Many different committees have oversight responsibilities over various aspects of the U.S.- EU commercial relationship. On the House side, these include the Committees on Agriculture, Energy and Commerce, Financial Services, Foreign Affairs, Judiciary, Transportation and Infrastructure, and Ways and Means. On the Senate side, these include the Committees on Agriculture, Banking, Commerce, Science, and Transportation, Finance, Foreign Relations, and Judiciary. A number of resolutions and hearings can be expected to take place in the second session of the 110th Congress on some of the issues raised in this chapter.

This chapter starts with background information and data on the commercial relationship and then discusses selective issues associated with trade in agricultural products, trade in services, and foreign direct investment. A concluding section assesses prospects for future cooperation and conflict.

BACKGROUND[2]

Trade and Investment Ties

The United States and the 27-member European Union (EU) share a huge, dynamic, and mutually beneficial economic partnership.[3] Not only is the EU-U.S. commercial relationship, what many call the transatlantic economy, the largest in the world, it is also arguably the most important. Agreement between the two partners in the past has been critical to making the world trade and financial system more open and efficient.[4]

The transatlantic economy dominates the world economy by its sheer size and prosperity. The combined population of the United States and EU now approaches 800 million people who generate a combined gross domestic product (GDP) of $26.8 trillion ($13.6 trillion in the EU and $13.2 trillion in the U.S.). This sum was equivalent to 56% of world production or GDP in 2006.[5]

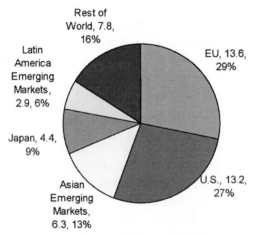

Source: IMF Global Financial Stability, Appendix Table 3.

Figure 1. World GDP in Trillions of U.S. Dollars, 2006

In addition, U.S. and EU international trade together accounts for just under 50% of world merchandise trade.[6] The combined weight of these two economic superpowers means that how the U.S. and EU manage their relationship and the difficult issues involving domestic regulations, competition policy, and foreign investment could well help determine how the rest of the world deals with similar issues.

Per capita incomes, averaging around $28,000 in the EU and $34,000 in the U.S. are among the highest in the world. In addition to having among the world's wealthiest populations, the United States and EU are major producers of advanced technologies and services. Both partners also have sophisticated and integrated financial sectors which facilitate a huge volume of capital flows across the Atlantic and throughout the world. For example, of an estimated $152 trillion in outstanding world assets of bonds, equities, and bank deposits in 2006, $106 trillion or 70% were held in the United States and EU.[7]

The United States and EU are also parties to the largest bilateral commercial relationship in the world. As shown in **Table 1**, the value of the two-way flow of goods, services, and income receipts from investments totaled $1.3 trillion in 2006. This sum means that almost $4.0 billion flows between the two partners everyday on the current account, the most comprehensive measure of international transactions.[8]

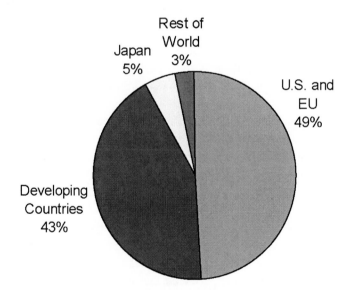

Source: IMF Direction of Trade Statistics.

Figure 2. World Exports and Imports of Goods, 2006

**Table 1. U.S. Current Account Balance with EU, 2006
(in billions of U.S. Dollars)**

Exports of Goods and Services	353.5
Imports of Goods and Services	459.4
Income Receipts	272.7
Income Payments	271.1
Unilateral Transfers (Net)	1.9
Total Current Account Flows	1,358.6

Source: CRS Report RL30608, *EU-U.S. Economic Ties: Framework, Scope, and Magnitude*, p. 7.

The United States and EU are each other's largest market for a host of goods and services, ranging from agricultural products to high tech goods and services. Large values of similar goods such as chemicals, transportation equipment, computers, and processed food as well as transportation and financial services are traded in record amounts. Within the EU, Germany, the United Kingdom, France, the Netherlands, and Italy are among the top 15 trading partners of the United States.[9]

Since 1993, the United States has been experiencing trade deficits with the EU. As shown in **Table 2**, these deficits peaked in 2005 at $123 billion. The trade deficit narrowed by 4.8% in 2006 to $117 billion and dropped by 8.4% to $107 billion in 2007.

Macroeconomic factors, such as differences in economic growth rates and exchange rates, rather than trade barriers or other structural attributes, are generally thought to explain most of the fluctuation in the U.S.-EU bilateral deficit. For example, the reduction in the trade deficit in 2006 and again in 2007 is being driven by a decline in the value of the dollar by nearly 40% against the euro and 30% against the British pound since 2002.[10]

Complaints about the decline of the dollar and rise of the euro, however, are being voiced in Europe. While a stronger euro improves the purchasing power of consumers by making imports cheaper and by keeping a lid on inflation, some governments are worried that a stronger currency can stymie exports and exacerbate trade deficits. French and Italian government leaders have expressed more concerns along these lines than German officials, a divide that could reflect differences in the competitiveness of these key countries within the euro zone.[11]

Table 2. U.S. Merchandise Trade Balance with the EU 27
(In billions of U.S. Dollars)

Year	U.S. Exports	U.S. Imports	Balance
2002	147	233	-86
2003	156	254	-98
2004	173	283	-110
2005	187	310	-123
2006	215	332	-117
2007	247	355	-107

Source: Global Trade Atlas.

Traditional trade barriers (tariffs and quotas) remain a problem in only a few selected areas such as agriculture, food, textiles and apparel. In these sectors, U.S. and EU tariffs still average between 10 and 20 percent ad valorem and help shield domestic producers from foreign competition.

Regulatory Cooperation

Instead of traditional barriers such as tariffs and quotas, non-tariff and regulatory barriers are increasingly recognized as the most significant trade and investment impediments to the creation of a more integrated transatlantic market. Prompted by this understanding, Germany's Chancellor Angela Merkel, upon assuming the rotating six-month Presidency of the EU in January 2007, advocated further liberalization of transatlantic trade and investment barriers by improving cooperation on reducing non-tariff and regulatory barriers to trade. The aim of such efforts is to reduce costs to businesses on both sides of the Atlantic, improve consumer welfare, and facilitate higher levels of economic growth.

Automotive safety standards are one example of how different regulations increase costs. For example, a U.S. citizen cannot go to Germany and purchase a BMW or Mercedes and import it directly into the United States because it does not meet U.S. safety standards. But if U.S. and German automakers had safety standards that were recognized by both the United States and EU, they could reduce their costs by not having to produce two different automobiles. The European Commission has estimated that further transatlantic liberalization of these kinds of regulatory barriers could lead to permanent gains of 3 to 3.5 percent in per capital gross domestic product on both sides of the Atlantic.

There have been a number of previous attempts to reduce remaining non-tariff and regulatory barriers to trade. These have included the New Transatlantic Agenda (1995), the Positive Economic Agenda (2002), the Transatlantic Economic Partnership (2004), and the Transatlantic Economic Agenda (2005). While each of these initiatives has made some progress towards reducing regulatory burdens, both European and U.S. companies heavily engaged in the transatlantic marketplace argue that the results have not proved materially significant.

In a departure from these past efforts that relied substantially on voluntary and non-binding dialogues among regulators with some political endorsement, the Merkel initiative proposed creating an overarching framework to provide greater commitment on the part of political leaders and greater accountability on the part of regulators. According to *Business Europe*, the EU's main business trade association, the initiative would require legislators and officials to take into account how new laws and regulations affect the transatlantic marketplace.[12] Merkel's proposal also covered issues such as public procurement, intellectual property, energy and the environment, financial markets and security, and innovation.

Building on and borrowing from the Merkel initiative, the April 2007 U.S.-EU Summit adopted a *Framework for Advancing Transatlantic Economic Integration*. The framework affirmed the importance of further deepening transatlantic economic integration, particularly through efforts to reduce or harmonize regulatory barriers to international trade and investment. A new institutional structure, a Transatlantic Economic Council (TEC), was established to advance the process of regulatory cooperation and barrier reduction.

The TEC is headed on both sides by ministerial-level appointees with cabinet rank.[13] Given that the two leaders are cabinet-level appointees, the TEC is expected to have high-level political support that previous efforts at economic integration may have lacked. Such clout, it is argued, is needed to persuade domestic regulators to yield some of their authorities or to better cooperate with their counterparts across the Atlantic in harmonizing regulatory approaches.[14]

The mandate of the TEC is to accelerate on-going efforts to reduce or harmonize regulatory barriers, in part, by including broader participation of stakeholders, including legislators, in the discussions and cooperative meetings. In particular, the framework document calls upon the TEC to draw upon the heads of the "existing transatlantic dialogues" to provide input and guidance on priorities for pursuing transatlantic economic integration. The existing transatlantic dialogues include the Transatlantic Legislators' Dialogue (the U.S. Congress-European Parliament exchange), the Transatlantic Business Dialogue, and the Transatlantic Consumers Dialogue.

The first meeting of the TEC took place on November 9, 2007 in Washington. At this meeting a report, prepared jointly by the Office of Management and Budget and the Secretariat-General of the European Commission, recommended including costs of regulation to foreign businesses in the cost-benefit analysis of new regulations.[15] While business groups see this initiative as an opportunity to resolve and or avoid trade disputes embedded in different regulatory approaches, some consumer groups are wary of such efforts to harmonize regulatory activities. The Transatlantic Consumer Dialogue, for example, warned that U.S. cost-benefit analyses of new regulations routinely overstate the costs and underestimate the benefits of regulations, to the detriment of consumers.[16]

The difficulty of harmonizing regulatory activities or resolving disputes embedded in regulatory differences was also underscored at the TEC meeting by failure to resolve a long-standing dispute involving U.S. exports of poultry to the EU. The EU ban is based on health safety concerns regarding the use of several antimicrobial agents used by U.S. processing plants. But U.S. industry and officials say the health safety concerns are being used as disguised trade barriers – a concern that is echoed in other U.S.-EU trade disputes rooted in regulatory differences.[17]

TRADE IN MANUFACTURED GOODS

Overview[18]

The EU as a unit is the largest merchandise trading partner of the United States. In 2006, the EU accounted for $196 billion of total U.S. merchandise exports (or 20.7%). Manufactured goods such as aircraft, and machinery of various kinds, including computers, integrated circuits, and office machine parts accounted for over 90% of this total. Similarly, manufactured goods such as passenger cars, machinery of various types, computers and components, office machinery, and organic chemicals accounted for over 88% of the $304 billion in U.S. imports (17.85% of total imports) from the EU.[19]

Table 3. Top U.S.-EU Exports and Imports by 2-Digit Commodity Classification, 2006

Top U.S. Exports to EU	Value (U.S. billions) and %	Top U.S Imports from the EU	Value (U.S. billions) and %
Machinery (non- electrical)	$40.5 (18.9%)	Machinery (non-electrical)	$53.0 (16.2%)
Optical and medical instruments	$21.8 (10.2%)	Vehicles	$41.0 (12.5%)
Electrical machinery	$21.6 (10.1%)	Pharmaceutical products	$28.0 (8.6%)
Pharmaceutical products	$14.6 (6.8%)	Organic chemicals	$26.4 (7.3%)
Organic chemicals	$11.5 (5.3%)	Electrical machinery	$18 (5.7%)
Totals	$110 (51.3%)		$166.4 (50.3%)

Source: CRS calculations based on Global Trade Atlas.

As shown in **Table 3**, a sizeable portion of U.S.-EU trade involves goods from the same industry, a phenomenon economists call intra-industry trade. This type of trade is particularly characteristic of large advanced economies that have similar resource endowments and levels of technology. Given that both the U.S. and EU produce goods under broadly similarly wage, safety, and environmental standards, each side concentrates on producing a narrower range of products at larger scale. By exploiting larger production runs of some sub-set of these goods, both sides are able to produce and trade at lower unit costs.

A significant attribute of intra-industry trade is that it tends not to generate the strong effects on the distribution of income that can occur when developed economies trade with less-developed economies. As a result, this kind of trade may prove less politically contentious due to broader sharing of the benefits garnered from rising productivity.[20]

While the vast majority of the trade in manufactured goods is transacted without major controversy, disputes do arise. The most prominent current dispute involves Airbus and Boeing and the manufacture and sale of commercial aircraft. An overview of this dispute is presented below.

In addition, numerous other barriers to market access are flagged by industry on both sides of the Atlantic. U.S. exporters, on the one hand, identify various EU member state policies governing pharmaceuticals and health care products and a new chemicals regulation as distorting trade. EU exporters to the United States, on the other hand, complain about technical regulations regarding consumer protection (including health and safety) and environmental protection, as well as additional requirements set by individual states. More detail on these complaints, as well as allegations of trade barriers affecting other sectors and industries, are contained in each side's annual trade barrier reports.[21]

Airbus-Boeing[22]

Claims and counter-claims concerning government support for the aviation industry have been a major source of friction in U.S.-EU relations over the past several decades. The disputes have focused primarily on EU member-state support for Airbus Industrie, now a part of Europe's largest aerospace firm, EADS (European Aeronautic Defense and Space Company). According to the Office of the U.S. Trade Representative (USTR), several European governments (France, U.K., Germany and Spain) have provided massive subsidies since 1967 to their aerospace firms to aid in the development, production, and marketing of the Airbus family of large civil aircraft. The U.S. has also accused the EU of providing other forms of support to gain an unfair advantage in this key sector, including equity infusions, debt forgiveness, debt rollovers, marketing assistance, and favored access to EU airports and airspace.[23]

For its part, the EU has long resisted U.S. charges and argued that for strategic and economic purposes it could not cede the entire passenger market to the Americans, particularly in the wake of the 1997 Boeing-McDonnell Douglas merger and the pressing need to maintain sufficient global competition. The Europeans have also counter-charged that their actions are justified because U.S. aircraft producers have benefitted from huge indirect governmental subsidies in the form of military and space contracts and government-sponsored aerospace research and development.[24]

The most recent round of this longstanding trade dispute stems from a May 30, 2005 WTO filing by the United States alleging that EU member states provided Airbus with illegal subsidies giving the firm an unfair advantage in the world market for large commercial jet aircraft. The following day the EC submitted its own request to the WTO claiming that Boeing had received illegal subsidies from the U.S. government. Two panels were established on October 17, 2005 (one handling the U.S. charges against Airbus and the other handling the EU's counterclaims against Boeing), and both panels have begun hearing the cases.

On September 26, 2007, the WTO dispute settlement panel heard oral arguments in the EU case (DS353) against the U.S. In the case, the EU claimed Boeing received about $24 billion in support in the form of "sham" contracts from the Department of Defense (DOD) and NASA, tax breaks from Illinois and Washington state, and bonds from Kansas. Furthermore, the EU charged that these subsidies and tax incentives cost Airbus $27 billion between 2004 and 2006 as the company either lost sales or had to sell its aircraft at lower prices.

U.S. trade officials rejected the EU claims that research contracts between Boeing and NASA or DOD are subsidies as defined by the WTO agreement on Subsidies and Countervailing Measures (ASCM). Rather than subsidies, the U.S. side argued that the contracts under question are research-for-pay arrangements in which Boeing gets paid for services rendered. During hearings on January 16 and 17, 2008, the panel asked the U.S. for more information to back its claim that NASA purchased $750 million in services from Boeing since 1992, not the $10 billion the EU is claiming.[25]

The EU case is in an earlier stage procedurally than the U.S. challenge to alleged Airbus subsidies (DS316), where an interim ruling may occur by the end of this year. The U.S. alleges that Airbus received $205 billion in illegal subsidies in the form of "launch aid" from the governments of Germany, United Kingdom, France, and Spain.

Much of the dispute stems from Airbus's December 2000 launch of a program to construct the world's largest commercial passenger aircraft, the Airbus A380. The A380 is being offered in several passenger versions seating between 500 and 800 passengers, and as a freighter. At the end of 2007, Airbus was listing 189 orders for the aircraft.[26] The project is believed to have cost about $18 billion, which includes some significant cost overruns. Airbus expects that its member firms will provide 60% of this sum, with the remaining 40% coming from subcontractors. State-aid from European governments is also a source of funding for Airbus member firms. State-aid is limited to one-third of the project's total cost by the 1992 Agreement on Government Support for Civil Aircraft between the United States and the EU (now repudiated by the United States, but not by the EU).

Shortly after the A380 project was announced, Boeing dropped its support of a competing new large aircraft. Boeing believes that the market for A380-size aircraft is limited. It has, therefore, settled on the concept of producing a new technology 250-seat aircraft, the 787, which is viewed as a replacement for 767-size aircraft.[27] The 787 is designed to provide point-to-point service on a wide array of possible international and domestic U.S. routes. The aircraft design incorporates features such as increased use of composite materials in structural elements and new engines, with the goal of producing an aircraft that is significantly more fuel efficient than existing aircraft types. Boeing formally launched the program in 2004 and obtained 56 firm orders during the remainder of 2004. By year-end 2007, the order book for the 787 had expanded dramatically to 817 aircraft.

To construct this aircraft Boeing has greatly expanded its use of non-U.S. subcontractors and non-traditional funding. For example, a Japanese group will provide approximately 35% of the funding for the project ($1.6 billion). In return this group will produce a large portion of the aircraft's structure and the wings (this will be the first time that a Boeing commercial product will use a non-U.S. built wing). Alenia of Italy is expected to provide $600 million and produce the rear fuselage of the aircraft. In each of these instances, the subcontractor is expected to receive some form of financial assistance from their respective governments. Other subcontractors are also taking large financial stakes in the new aircraft. The project is also expected to benefit from state and local tax and other incentives. Most notable among these is $3.2 billion of such incentives from the state of Washington. Many of these non-traditional funding arrangements are specifically cited by the EU in its WTO complaint as being illegal subsidies.

Whether the prospect of protracted WTO litigation provides an incentive for the United States and the EU to resolve the dispute bilaterally remains to be seen. To date the two sides have wrangled over a host of procedural issues, but have not been negotiating on a possible settlement to the dispute. In October 2007, Airbus Americas Chairman Allan McArtor publically spoke about the value of a negotiated settlement that would set the rules for subsidizing the development of large civil aircraft along the lines of the 1992 Civil Aircraft agreement. Some analysts believe that any Airbus negotiating effort along these lines may be driven by the needs of Airbus parent EADS to complete a corporate restructuring, and find launch aid and other capital to complete development of its new A3 50, which is designed to compete with the 787. In addition, there may be a view that Airbus has more to lose than Boeing from WTO rulings in the pending cases. At the same time, the impact of the Air Force's awarding to EADS, parent company of Airbus, the contract for the cargo refueling program could have some bearing.[28]Other analysts speculate that Airbus' weakened business condition brought on by the delivery delays of its jumbo A380 plane may also be a reason why it may be more inclined now to settle the case. On the other hand, Boeing officials continue to publically maintain that they are not interested in settling the case. Rather they express confidence in the strength of the U.S. WTO case which alleges that launch aid for Airbus is a prohibited subsidy under the ACSM.

TRADE IN AGRICULTURAL AND PRIMARY PRODUCTS[29]

Overview

The United States and the EU-27, the world's leading producers and exporters of agricultural products, also are significant markets for each other's agricultural exports. The EU is the United States' fourth largest agricultural export market. In FY2007, U.S. agricultural exports to the EU amounted to $8.0 billion according to the U.S. Department of Agriculture, while U.S. agricultural imports from the EU totaled just under $15.0 billion. Tree nuts (almonds, walnuts, pistachios, pecans, etc.) are the largest single component of U.S. agricultural exports to the EU, accounting for more than $1.4 billion in 2007. The next largest categories are soybeans, tobacco, and wine and beer. The largest commodity categories of U.S. agricultural imports from the EU are wine and beer (more than $4.8 billion in 2007), essential oils (e.g, peppermint or spearmint oils, that are widely used for flavoring or fragrances), cheese and other dairy products, and snack foods, including chocolate.

Among factors affecting U.S.-EU agricultural trade flows have been disputes over trade in meats from animals produced with growth-promoting hormones; differences in consumer attitudes and regulatory requirements for genetically modified organisms (GMOs) such as genetically modified varieties of soybeans and corn; and differences over legal protections accorded to geographical indications for agricultural products.

Meat Hormones

In a January 1998 ruling, the Appellate Body (AB) of the World Trade Organization (WTO), upheld an earlier panel ruling which found that the EU had violated the WTO's Agreement on the Application of Sanitary and Phytosanitary Measures (the SPS Agreement) by prohibiting imports of U.S. meats and other products derived from animals raised with growth-promoting hormones. The panel and the AB concurred that the EU had not conducted an assessment of the risks to consumers of eating hormone treated meat. The AB, however, left open the possibility that the EU could conduct another risk assessment. When the EU declined to comply with the WTO ruling by lifting its hormone ban, the United States, in July 1999, sought and obtained WTO authorization to impose restrictive tariffs on imports from the EU worth $116.8 million annually. Subsequent efforts to negotiate a compensation agreement that would have enlarged the EU's quota for non-hormone treated beef from the United States in exchange for lifting the punitive duties were not successful.

In October of 2003, the EU announced that its Scientific Committee on Veterinary Measures had concluded that one of the six hormones in question — oestradiol 17 — should be considered carcinogenic and that for five others the current state of knowledge did not make it possible for the Committee to provide a quantitative assessment of their risks to consumers. As a result, the EU argued, its ban on hormone-treated meat was justified, and the United States (and Canada, which also had challenged the EU ban) should lift punitive duties. The United States and Canada refused on grounds that the scientific evidence produced by the EU Committee was not new information nor did it establish a risk to consumers from eating hormone-treated meat. In January 2005, the EU requested the establishment of a WTO dispute panel to determine if the United States and Canada are in violation of WTO rules by maintaining the prohibitive tariffs in light of the EU's claim that it has complied with the panel decision. The establishment of the panel was delayed, however, in part due to disagreement among the disputants about its membership. The panel was ultimately established in June 2005. In January 2006, the panel announced that because of the complexity of the issues and the procedural matters involved it could not deliver its decision until October 2006. The report was further delayed, again according to WTO officials, because of the complexity of the issues involved.

A final panel report, circulated to the parties on December 21, 2007, reportedly upheld a confidential interim panel ruling circulated in July 2007.[30] In the final report, the panel ruled that the EU's legislation with respect to the ban on hormone- treated meat did not comply with the SPS Agreement. The SPS agreement requires that food safety measures applied to imports be based on a risk assessment According to the SPS Agreement, if provisional measures to protect food health and safety are imposed, WTO members are obliged to seek a more objective risk assessment in a reasonable period of time. Reports indicate that the panel thought that the EU had not complied with the SPS

Agreement requirement to seek a more objective risk assessment in a reasonable period of time. The panel also found that the United States (and co-complainant Canada) did not follow WTO dispute settlement rules and procedures to determine if their sanctions were still justified. WTO dispute settlement rules require a determination by the WTO that a country is not complying with the rules before enacting sanctions. Nevertheless, the decision will allow the United States to keep in place its prohibitive tariffs on such EU products as Roquefort cheese, goose liver, fruit juices, mustard, and pork products.

Approvals of Genetically Modified Organisms (GMOs)

The United States, Canada, and Argentina in May 2003 initiated a challenge in the WTO to the EU's *de facto* moratorium on approving new agricultural biotechnology products, in effect since 1998. Although the EU effectively lifted the moratorium in May 2004 by approving a genetically modified corn variety, the three countries contend the EU approval process for GMOs violates the SPS Agreement and is discriminatory and not transparent. The moratorium, according to U.S. estimates, costs U.S. corn growers some $300 million in exports to the EU annually. U.S. growers plant genetically modified corn mainly for weed and pest control. They do not segregate GMO from non-GMO varieties, because the U.S. regulatory system recognizes them (once approved for commercialization) as substantially equivalent to traditional varieties. The EU moratorium, U.S. officials contend, threatened U.S. agricultural exports not only to the EU, but also to other parts of the world where the EU approach to regulating agricultural biotechnology is taking hold. The EU approach presumes that the products of biotechnology are inherently different than their conventional counterparts and should be more closely regulated. Other exports, e.g., corn gluten feed and soybeans, also have been adversely affected by negative consumer attitudes in the EU about GMOs.

On February 7, 2006, the WTO dispute panel, in its report, ruled that a moratorium had existed, that bans on EU-approved genetically engineered crops in six EU member countries violated WTO rules, and that the EU failed to ensure that its approval procedures were conducted without "undue delay." The dispute panel's ruling, however, dismissed several other U.S. and co-complainant claims including claims that EU approval procedures were not based on appropriate risk assessment; that the EU unfairly applied different risk assessment standards for genetically engineered processing agents; and that the EU had unjustifiably discriminated between WTO members. The panel made no recommendations to the EU as to how to bring its practices in line with WTO rules, nor does the ruling appear to require the EU to change its regulatory framework for approving GE products. The panel did not address such sensitive issues as whether GE products are safe or whether an EU moratorium on GE approvals continued to exist. The EU did not appeal the panel's decision, but announced instead its intention to comply with the decisions of the panel. By mutual agreement, the United States and the EU set November 21, 2007 as the end of a reasonable period of time for implementation of the panel's report.

The "reasonable period of time" for EU compliance with the dispute panel's ruling was subsequently extended by mutual agreement to January 11, 2008. On that date, the U.S. Trade Representative announced that, while it was reserving its rights to retaliate, it would hold off seeking a compliance ruling. USTR indicated that it would work with the EU to normalize trade in biotechnology products.[31] No deadline was announced for making a decision with respect to retaliation. According to USTR, the EU's observance of a set of benchmarks, not yet announced, would determine the United States' next move in WTO dispute settlement.

The impact of the U.S.-EU GMO case is uncertain. Given widespread opposition to GMOs by EU consumers and environmentalists, it seems unlikely that U.S. exports of such products would increase in the near term as a result of the panel ruling and the U.S.-EU effort to "normalize" trade in GMO products. U.S. officials suggest, however, that since the panel's decision affirms that countries must conform their biotech regulations to international obligations, the trade impact in countries that have not yet adopted comprehensive biotech regulations could be positive. The decision also could strengthen the hand of the European Commission in dealing with member countries that maintain marketing/import bans on GMOs or that are contemplating biotech regulations stricter than those being implemented by the Commission. However, Austria and Hungary are still maintaining WTO-prohibited bans on genetically modified corn varieties approved by the EU Commission. More recently, France announced that it was invoking a safeguard prohibition on cultivation of a genetically engineered corn variety, the only biotech corn approved for cultivation in the EU. The EU Commission has 60 days in which to review and decide on the validity of this safeguard action.

Protection of Geographical Indications (GIs)

GI's are place names (or words associated with a place) used to identify products (for example, Champagne, Tequila or Roquefort) which have a particular quality, reputation or other characteristic because they come from that place. The EU accords greater protection to GIs than does the United States and some other countries. As a result the issue of protecting GIs has arisen in WTO dispute settlement and in agriculture negotiations. In June 1999, the United States requested consultations with the EU over its regulations for the protection of GIs which the United States said discriminated against U.S. GIs. Consultations failed to resolve the dispute, and in 2003, the United States requested and won the establishment of a panel to adjudicate the dispute. The United States charged that the EU regulations violated the WTO Agreement on Trade-Related Aspects of Intellectual Property Rights (TRIPS) by failing to provide national treatment (i.e., imports treated the same as domestic products) for U.S. GI's within the EU and by failing to provide sufficient protection to pre-existing trademarks that are identical or similar to European GIs.

The EU regulation required that GIs from other countries could be registered in the EU only if the country in question accorded protection equivalent to that available in the EU. According to the United States this "reciprocity" provision in the EU (e.g., maintenance of a registry of names) was in violation of the national treatment requirement in TRIPS. The United States complained also about permitting coexistence of names (for example, *Budweiser* and Czech names that in translation are the same) as they might confuse consumers and call into question pre-existing trademarks rights such as those *Budweiser* has in several EU countries. The panel sided with the United States on the issue of national treatment, but with the EU on the issue of coexistence rights, which the panel said should be limited to GIs that already appear on the EU register, but not to translations. This decision, admittedly narrow, has particular importance for *Budweiser* which felt threatened by the ability of Czech producers to appropriate its trademark in translation following the Czech Republic's accession to the EU (May 2004).

The EU issued regulations in March 2006 to bring its protection of GIs into compliance with the WTO decision. Under the new regulations, non-EU companies will not have to apply for registration of GIs through their national governments; producers themselves can make these applications. The changed regulations also eliminate the requirements that non-EU applicants for GI protection must be from countries that make equivalent guarantees on their home market and for third countries to give EU GIs the same level of protection. Although U.S. business interests has generally welcomed the new regulations, USTR has indicated that, from its point of view, there may be some issues with respect to the protection accorded existing trademarks that need clarification or resolution.

The decision and the new regulations could have limited near-term commercial implications if U.S. producers of products associated with place names (e.g., Idaho potatoes or Florida oranges) seek registration in the EU. The decision also may have implications for Doha round negotiations on GIs. USTR has maintained that existing WTO intellectual property protections for GIs are sufficient and priority should be placed on WTO members meeting current obligations and not on expanding GI protection in the WTO Doha negotiations. The EU, however, continues to push for expanded GI protection for agricultural and other products in the current trade round and is linking agreements on GIs to negotiations of U.S. priorities in the round such as curbing trade-distorting domestic support, eliminating export subsidies, and cutting agricultural tariffs.

TRADE IN SERVICES

Overview[32]

Like all developed market economies, the United States and EU are predominantly service economies. The service sector, which includes a range of economic activities including banking and insurance, and other financial services to express delivery, transportation, information technology, telecommunications and professional services such as accounting, engineering and legal services, as well as entertainment and wholesale and retail trade, accounts for over 75% of employment and output in both the U.S. and EU.[33]

The U.S. and the EU are the largest exporters of services, accounting for about 50% of world trade in services. The EU is also the largest U.S. trade partner in services. In 2006 U.S. exports of services to Europe totaled $164 billion, or 41% of overall U.S. exports of services. U.S. service imports from Europe in the same year totaled $137 billion (or 44% of total imports), giving the U.S. a trade surplus of $27 billion in services trade. At the same time, sales of services by U.S. affiliates in Europe and European affiliates in the U.S. tend to be about double the amount that is traded.[34]

While the U.S. federal government and individual states still impose selective barriers on a range of business, professional, legal, and transport services, the market for services in the EU tends to be more regulated and fragmented by different member states policies. Nevertheless, most EU Member States are actively deregulating service sectors, although at varying rates, and the European Commission has approached liberalization in a comprehensive way through implementation of a Services Directive that was passed in 2004. In addition to these efforts, liberalization of services barriers are being dealt with multilaterally in the context of the Doha Round and bilaterally in the context of efforts to enhance the market integration of selective service sectors. Two such efforts – the Air Transport Agreement and Financial Regulatory Dialogue – are discussed below.

Air Transport Agreement[35]

The United States and European Union signed a first-stage Air Transport Agreement at the U.S.-EU summit of April 30, 2007. The Agreement, which had been under negotiation for four years, will replace existing bilateral agreements between the United States and individual EU member states and will substantially liberalize the transatlantic air services market. Congressional approval of this Executive Agreement is not required. The accord will allow every U.S. and EU airline to fly between any city in the EU and any city in the United States with no restrictions on the number of flights, routes, and aircraft provided they can reach agreements with airports for landing rights, gates, and counter space. It also will open to competition London's Heathrow Airport, where landing rights have been restricted to two British and two U.S. carriers (providing those airlines wishing to serve the airport are able to obtain takeoff/landing slots from incumbent airlines).

The Air Transport Agreement takes effect March 30, 2008. The European Commission predicts that the agreement will lower airline fares on transatlantic travel, expand the number of passengers by 50% over the next five years, and create 80,000 new jobs.[36] But the agreement is not without controversy. Many Europeans argue that it is not balanced because it does not give European carriers the right to fly between U.S. cities and maintains limits on EU ownership of U.S. airlines. While most U.S. airlines support the agreement, the major U.S. unions representing pilots, machinists, flight attendants, and baggage handlers oppose it on the grounds that it will lead to a further erosion of jobs, benefits, and wages.[37]

Air services between the U.S. and EU presently operate on the basis of bilateral agreements between individual member states of the EU and the U.S. Accordingly, European airlines can fly to the United States only from the countries where they are based as long as the U.S. has reached a bilateral agreement with the country in question. Air France, for example, can fly to a U.S. destination only from a French airport under a bilateral aviation agreement.

These bilateral agreements contain provisions that the European Court of Justice determined in November 2002 to be incompatible with Community law. In particular, the Court determined that some bilateral agreements with the U.S. discriminated between different EU airlines, breaking internal market rules. The Court ruling, in turn, created an impetus for negotiating a new legal framework for U.S.-EU aviation relations. The EU objective in the negotiations was the creation of a single market for air transport in which investment could flow freely and in which European and U.S. airlines would be able to provide air services without any restriction, including in the domestic markets of both parties.

Achievement of the EU objective in full would require significant legislative changes in the United States, in particular the removal of some existing legal restrictions on foreign ownership and control of U.S. airlines and cabotage (which restricts foreign airlines from making flights directly between U.S. cities). Because these issues remain very sensitive politically in the United States, the EU accepted that cabotage would not be included in a first-stage agreement if meaningful progress was made towards removal of U.S. foreign investment restrictions.[38]

While the air transport agreement did provide separate new investment regulations that eliminate for EU airlines numerous existing administrative rules that limit foreign participation in U.S. airline management, the requirement that foreign nationals not own more than 25% of the voting stock of a U.S. airline remained. Thus, the EU can be expected to take up the issues of cabotage and remaining restrictions on foreign investment in the second-stage agreement scheduled to begin no later than May 30, 2008.[39]

Financial Services Dialogue[40]

The financial market's regulatory dialogue between the United States and the European Union began in 2002. Most of the issues in the initial discussions are still ongoing, however, the discussions today are more narrowly focused.

Earlier discussions were seeking more effective financial regulations in response to the break down of corporate governance as a result of a number of corporate scandals and on implementing the European Union's Financial Services Action Plan and the United States' Sarbanes-Oxley Act. The antiterrorism financing discussions are now narrowed to discussions between the European Commission and the U.S. Treasury Department on the protection of personal data on money wire transfers. EU discussions of establishing a Single European Payments Area have been accompanied by both sides reaching an agreement to open the European Union's markets to U.S. financial services companies. The following is a brief update of the United States and the European Union's financial markets regulatory discussions on harmonizing accounting standards, protecting personal financial data privacy, and opening European financial services markets to U.S. firms. Some other financial services issues being discussed are Basel II capital accord, and the sub-prime crisis, which is negatively impacting financial institutions on both sides of the Atlantic.

U.S.-EU Accounting Standards

For corporate governance, accounting standards are critical tools in enforcing supervisory control over corporations and financial institutions. The Securities and Exchange Commission (SEC) requires all publicly traded firms listed on the U.S. stock exchanges to use U.S. Generally Accepted Accounting Principles (GAAP) in reporting their financial statements to the SEC. The European Union, on the other hand, adopted the International Financial Reporting Standard (IFRS). The main difference is that GAAP is a rule- based standard, while the IFRS is a principles-based standard, which is more flexible than GAAP. With EU and U.S. firms listed in each other's securities markets, it is important to have significant commonality in accounting standards. Furthermore, the implementation of the Sarbanes-Oxley Act has caused the European Commission to engage in a regulatory dialogue with U.S. authorities concerning equivalence in corporate governance.[41] On March 12, 2004, the European Commission announced that the SEC would recognize foreign companies' use of the International Financial Reporting Standards when reporting financial results, with a process to reconcile differences. While the SEC has allowed foreign companies to use the IFRS standard, the SEC has not allowed U.S. firms to use the IFRS, because the IFRS is not as comprehensive as GAAP.

The SEC and European Commission are in ongoing accounting standards talks. In July 2007, the SEC proposed dropping the U.S. GAAP reconciliation process in the 2004 agreement as long as EU firms use the International Financial Reporting Standards, and the SEC and EU continue to make progress in reconciling their accounting systems. The European Commission objected to keeping the reconciliation requirement. The SEC argued that the EU Commission's current stance would undermine true convergence and accounting compatibility for financial reporting, because each EU-member state has flexibility to modify the IFRS to accommodate national accounting practices. Filings made under the "German IFRS," "Dutch IFRS," and "Belgian IFRS" would not be the same. U.S. accounting firms generally support the SEC position arguing that jurisdictional differences in IFRS need to be avoided.[42]

Antiterrorism Financing and Personal Financial Data Protection

The European Commission's Justice and Home Affairs directorate is in talks with the U.S. Treasury Department concerning the protection of personal financial data in U.S.–EU antiterrorist financing enforcement. In June 2006, press reports revealed that U.S. authorities had been accessing the personal data of wire transfers handled by the Society for Worldwide Interbank Financial Telecommunication (SWIFT). SWIFT is a cooperative that supplies messaging services and interface software to 8,100 banks and financial institutions in more than 207 countries. The U.S. Treasury Department has argued that collecting and retaining wire transfer information from SWIFT is a crucial element in ongoing terrorism investigations. European data protection officials disagreed strongly, accusing SWIFT of violating the EU data privacy protection directive (law) by turning over millions of transaction records to U.S. officials. The EU data protection directive restricts transfer of data to countries that do not have privacy standards that the EU deems adequate. The EU does not deem the United States' privacy standards adequate.

While the talks continued with the U.S. Treasury Department and the EU Commission, SWIFT announced significant changes to its operations to address the antiterrorist financing personal data protection issue. On October 4, 2007, the SWIFT board approved a plan to add a new operation center in Switzerland by the end of 2009 that will allow all intra-European financial transfers not involving the United States to be handled completely within the European economic area. Currently, SWIFT has operation centers in Europe and the United States to handle intra-European and transatlantic transfers. Transfers are processed simultaneously at both the European and U.S. locations, including those conducted among exclusively European countries. While the protracted negotiation continues, on June 28, 2007, the United

States and the European Commission agreed to allow U.S. antiterrorism authorities, mostly in the U.S. Treasury Department, to use SWIFT data for their investigations, while protecting EU citizens' data privacy. However, SWIFT is required to inform EU customers that their data could be given to U.S. authorities, and that EU citizens should apply for their membership in the EU-U.S. safe harbor program. The safe harbor program was negotiated in 2000 to provide a way for entities to transfer personal data from EU-member states to the United States. It is a self-certifying program that confirms that the entities (now citizens) have adhered to a set of data privacy protection principles. Under the safe harbor program, EU citizens' privacy is protected because the U.S. firms involved in these data transactions have agreed to principles of conduct that protect the privacy of the transactions. The EU/U.S. negotiating team was expected to complete their work in the third quarter of 2007, but there was no formal announcement that they met that expectation.

Opening EU Markets to U.S. Financial Services Companies

While the United States and the European Union reached an agreement on September 2006 to open European markets to U.S. services companies including financial services, the European Commission sued 24 member states for failing to implement a financial services directive. This directive would open the financial services markets to both the United States as well as EU member states. Specifically, the European Commission took legal action against 24 European Union member states for failure to implement the necessary laws and regulations to break down national laws that prevent cross-border capital markets to operate efficiently. The Commission, the executive body of the EU, took legal action because only three member states – the United Kingdom, Romania and Ireland – met the January 31, 2006 deadline to implement the Markets in Financial Instruments Directive (MiFID). Consequently, the EU financial services markets remain restrictive.

U.S. firms would have to comply with one set of laws and regulations instead of 27 (the three that have enacted the national laws and the 24 that have been sued). The MiFID was to establish the single passport system, which would allow investment firms to operate throughout the EU under the supervision of the financial services regulator of the member state where the firm is based. Currently, like the U.S. financial firms operating in the EU, EU financial services firms must abide by the regulation of the member state in which they are doing business. The deadline set in the MiFID was November 1, 2007. The failure of the European national governments to implement MiFID legislation places the financial services markets' unification plans at risk. According to the European Commission, "In this situation there is a risk that member states can face legal action by private parties who might claim damages for losses incurred because of late implementation of national legislation."[43] The risk of such damage claims is because financial firms throughout the EU have incurred major expenditures in preparation for the implementation of the MiFID. The U.K. Financial Services Authority has estimated the changes being made by financial firms in the UK could run up to $2 billion.

The EU/U.S. agreement to open EU markets to U.S. financial services firms while its financial services markets remain fragmented is of limited value to U.S. firms wanting to expand internationally, because of the high cost of operating under 25 countries' laws and regulations instead of one. Supporting this argument, in a report published September 20, 2007, the Organization for Economic Cooperation and Development (OECD) urged the European Union to address the integration of Europe's banking and financial sectors.

Other U.S.-EU Financial Services Issues

Several additional areas of EU/U.S. financial services regulation have yet to be resolved. Among them are the implementation of the Basel II capital accord, and EU regulatory response to the sub- prime market crisis.

- The United States is set to implement its version of the Basel II capital accord, while the EU has implemented its Basel II accord more than a year ago. Basel II is an international agreement that provides a framework for determining the minimum capital that depository institutions are required to hold as a cushion against insolvency. Basel II attempts to improve the risk sensitivity of Basel I (the current capital accord) in determining required capital. Countries whose banks are allowed to hold less capital have a competitive advantage over banks that are required to hold more capital. Analysts expect some new negotiations between the U.S. and the EU to level the playing field when the U.S. Basel II is fully implemented. The U.S. version could advantage or disadvantage EU banks that are in competition with U.S. banks.
- Many EU banks have experienced a liquidity crisis due to the U.S. subprime mortgage foreclosures and defaults, a situation that was temporarily remedied by the European central bank (ECB) providing needed liquidity to these troubled institutions. For example, the ECB

had to provide a German bank a \$23 billion line of credit because of losses it incurred from defaulted loans in the U.S. subprime market. The impact of the U.S. subprime crisis on European institutions has brought calls for a European Commission investigation of U.S. rating agencies such as Standard & Poors and Moody's for conflict of interest. In response, U.S. Senator Richard Shelby on August 20, 2007 urged the European Union to avoid unnecessary regulation of financial services as a result of the deteriorating subprime collapse.[44] U.S. remedies to the subprime crisis may result in legal actions from European investors. For example, U.S. Treasury Secretary Paulson's plan to freeze certain mortgage interest rates would expose European investors to losses that they might not find acceptable.

FOREIGN DIRECT INVESTMENT

Overview[45]

The fact that each side has a major ownership stake in the other's market may be the most distinctive aspect of the transatlantic economy. At the end of 2006, the total stock of two-way direct investment reached \$2.2 trillion (composed of \$1.1 trillion of U.S. direct investment in EU countries and \$1.1 trillion of EU direct investments in the U.S.), making U.S. and European companies the largest investors in each other's market. Roughly 47% of all U.S. foreign direct investment is located in Europe, while EU member states supply 62% of foreign direct investment in the United States. As viewed in **Tables 4** and **5**, these high magnitudes have remained constant over the past eight years.

This massive amount of ownership of companies in each other's markets translates into billions of dollars of sales, profits, production, and expenditures on research and development. In addition, an estimated six to seven million Americans are employed by European affiliates operating in the United States and almost an equal number of EU citizens work for American companies in Europe.[46]

As these data might suggest, both the U.S. and EU have policies that are receptive to FDI. In theory, both sides appear to acknowledge that there is nothing to gain from protectionist investment policies. Differences exist, however, in term of remaining irritants and barriers on both sides of the Atlantic.

A good portion of FDI activity involves the acquisition of new plant and equipment, the bulk of it centers on merger and acquisition (M&A) activity. EU M&A activity in the United States, for example, totaled $114 billion in 2006, up from $57 billion in 2005.[47] While M&A activity is not controversial per se, from time to time regulation of business activities through application of competition or antitrust polices has created transatlantic tensions. This came to light in 2002 when Europe prevented General Electric from merging with Honeywell. Most recently, the EU's decision on Microsoft's alleged abuse of its dominant position heightened concerns over different approaches to antitrust law in the U.S. and Europe. These main differences and their significance are discussed below.

Table 4. Foreign Direct Investment in the United States on a Historical Cost Basis, Percentage Share

Region	1999	2000	2001	2002	2003	2004	2005	2006
EU*	60	64	64	64	61	62	62	62
Asia	19	15	14	14	14	15	14	15
Canada	9	9	8	7	7	8	10	9
Latin America	4	4	4	4	6	5	4	4

*EU 15 (1999-2003); EU-25 (2004-2006)
Source: Various editions of the Survey of Current Business

Table 5. U.S. Direct Investment Position Abroad on a Historical Cost Basis, Percentage Share

Region	1999	2000	2001	2002	2003	2004	2005	2006
EU*	46	46	46	47	48	49	47	47
Asia	16	16	16	17	16	17	18	18
Canada	10	10	10	10	11	10	11	10
Latin America	21	20	20	18	17	16	17	17

* EU 15 (1999-2003); EU-25 (2004-2006)
Source: Various editions of the Survey of Current Business

U.S. and EU Perspectives on Antitrust and Competition[48]

Fifteen years ago, few national or super-national jurisdictions had competition laws and even fewer of them enforced those laws. Today, more than 100 jurisdictions have such laws, which increasingly are being enforced. The United States has played a significant role in encouraging the spread of competition laws, and now has a strong interest in promoting convergence toward sound enforcement of those laws.[49]

Multinational firms, competition agencies, and antitrust practitioners (attorneys and economists) have been especially interested in fostering convergence between the United States and the European Union. A number of conferences and symposiums on both sides of the Atlantic have addressed the issue, and American and European researchers continue to analyze the impact of agency policies and specific decisions.[50] Although there is general agreement that the United States and the EU are moving toward substantial antitrust convergence in the areas of cartels and horizontal mergers, differences remain with respect to enforcement of the unilateral conduct of dominant or monopoly firms (often as they relate to vertical relationships) – such as bundled discounts, loyalty discounts, tying, refusals to deal, exclusive dealing, and predatory pricing.[51] These differences reflect differences in the underlying laws, as well as in important historical developments.

That the United States and EU may, on occasion, reach differing conclusions about the competition/antitrust lawfulness of an entity's activities is understandable when one examines the language of their respective, relevant statutes. U.S. law addresses "monopolization," while EU law addresses "dominance."

"Monopolization" in the United States

Section 2 of the Sherman Act (15 U.S.C. § 2) prohibits "monopolization" (a situation in which a monopolist couples its monopoly status with behavior designed to unlawfully exploit, maintain, or enhance its market position) and "attempted monopolization" (a situation in which an entity unlawfully attempts to secure a market monopoly).[52] A shorthand definition of "monopoly" is "the power to control prices or exclude competition."[53] While it is not illegal for a company to have or to seek to achieve a monopoly position, "the willful acquisition or maintenance of monopoly power ... by the use of exclusionary conduct"[54] is illegal.

In the United States:

- vertical restraints are no longer considered per se illegal, but rather are judged under the rule of reason (i.e., a method of antitrust analysis under which a technical antitrust violation may be saved by balancing the anti-competitive results against any pro-competitive effects), and in recent years such restraints rarely have been successfully challenged;
- predatory pricing (the practice of a firm with market power temporarily selling a product at a below-cost price with the intent of driving competitors out of the market or keeping potential entrants out of the market, and raising its prices again when those objectives have been largely achieved and it is, therefore, able to recoup its losses) rarely is challenged by the antitrust agencies;
- claims that specific refusals to deal, monopoly leveraging, or refusals to provide access to essential facilities tend to be met with some skepticism by the antitrust agencies and courts.

Those unilateral practices are not generally prosecuted because either they are not deemed to harm competition or the allegation itself is unprovable.

Consumers are presumed to benefit from the existence of largely competitive markets. The impact on excluded *competitors* is relevant only insofar as it affects the fate of *competition*:

> [t]he antitrust injury requirement obligates [complainants] to demonstrate, as a threshold matter, "that the challenged conduct has had an actual adverse effect on competition as a whole in the relevant market; to prove it has been harmed as an individual competitor will not suffice."[55]
> ... it is axiomatic that the antitrust laws were passed for "the protection of *competition, not competitors.* "[56]

In scrutinizing the effects of a firm's actions on competition, U.S. courts have increasingly turned to what supporters call "economic principles"[57] and what detractors call "the conservative economic scholarship of the 'Chicago School'"[58] to focus Section 2 on the consumer welfare and economic efficiency effects of those actions. Under this microeconomic model, there should not be antitrust intervention unless the activity is likely to diminish aggregate consumer wealth. Exploitation of monopoly power is not a violation of Section 2 unless there is harm to consumers.

There is debate among economists, however, about what constitutes "consumer welfare" or "consumer wealth" or "harm to consumers." Chicago School economists tend to construe these concepts broadly, to include society's wealth as a whole, that is, to include the wealth of both consumers and producers. Thus, an activity that decreases the welfare of end-user consumers, but increases the welfare of producers by a greater amount, would be viewed as increasing total consumer welfare. In contrast, more liberal economists tend to construe "consumer welfare" and "consumer wealth" and "harm to consumers" more narrowly and some argue that antitrust analysis should focus on "consumer surplus," which measures the effect on end-user consumers only.

The Chicago School approach adopted by the U.S. courts has been characterized by one observer as an "outcome-oriented definition of competition and impairment,"[59] with a single relevant outcome measure – the impact on consumer welfare as that term is broadly defined. It has an important corollary: Section 2 has not been interpreted to provide protection to smaller rivals from aggressive competition by monopolists unless consumers are being harmed.

"Dominance" in the EU

In contrast, Article 82 (as amended) of the Treaty of Rome that established the European Community reads:

> Any abuse by one or more undertakings of a *dominant position* within the common market or in a substantial part of it shall be prohibited as incompatible with the common market in so far as it may affect trade between Member States.[60]

Pursuant to Article 82, such abuse may consist of:

- directly or indirectly imposing unfair purchase or selling prices or other unfair trading conditions;
- limiting production, markets or technical development to the prejudice of consumers;
- applying dissimilar conditions to equivalent transactions with other trading parties, thereby placing them at a competitive disadvantage; and

- making the conclusion of contracts subject to acceptance by the other parties of supplementary obligations which, by their nature or according to commercial usage, have no connection with the subject of such contracts.

Given the references to unfairness and competitive disadvantage, Article 82 has been interpreted to be concerned with market effects on competitors as well as on consumers. In evaluating dominant firms' actions, the EU has tended to employ "post-Chicago School" economic models that focus on strategic game theory and are not as skeptical about the potential for competitive injury as are the Chicago School models relied on in the United States.[61] A determination of whether there is harm to competition "asks whether the practice interferes with and degrades the market mechanism."[62]

One observer has voiced concern that "enforcement of the law under a 'protection of the market' paradigm can spill over into protection of competitors."[63] There is no consensus, however, as to whether that has occurred in the EU, though case law in the EU has been harsh on dominant firms that employ loyalty rebates, bundled discounts on multiple products, exclusive dealing, tying arrangements, refusals to deal, and refusals to license, while such activities are rarely found to be illegal – and in some cases are in effect per se legal – in the United States.[64]

Impact of different laws and philosophies

Although both the United States and the EU look toward consumer welfare as the hoped-for end product of their enforcement actions,[65] their philosophies about the best means to arrive at that goal do not always agree. The U.S. monopolization statute is based on the belief that consumers benefit most when markets function competitively, and so focuses on the effects of an entity's actions on competition and markets rather than on effects on competitors.[66] Article 82, on the other hand, appears more compatible with the notion that consumer benefit will best be realized when a dominant firm's adverse effects on competitors are minimized or prevented. Further, "abuse ... of a dominant position" may not always equate to "monopolization."[67] Moreover, as explained earlier, the United States employs a broader concept of consumer welfare when evaluating the effect of a firm's behavior, incorporating benefits to the producer, even if these come at the expense of consumers.

Accordingly, there have been times when U.S. authorities have found the actions of a dominant firm – even a monopolist – to be legal, or have agreed to a settlement that imposed relatively limited restrictions on a dominant firm, or have approved a merger, while EU authorities have found those same actions to be illegal, or have imposed far more restrictive settlement terms on the dominant firm, or have disapproved a merger. Notable examples include complaints brought against Microsoft and the proposed merger between General Electric and Honeywell.

In 2004, the EU imposed on Microsoft both conduct remedies and a substantial fine for the bundling of its operating system and media software. (The European Commission began its investigation of Microsoft after receiving a complaint from Sun Microsystems, a multinational U.S. company that competed with Microsoft, alleging that Microsoft was refusing to supply necessary interoperability information.) Most of the Commission's decision was subsequently upheld by the European Court of First Instance.[68] The U.S. Department of Justice also brought a complaint against Microsoft, alleging that Microsoft had unlawfully attempted to "extend its operating system into other software markets." But the settlement it reached with Microsoft to "restrain anti-competitive conduct" was less far-reaching, and was unsuccessfully challenged by several states as not being stringent enough.[69] In January 2008 the EU announced, also subsequent to the complaint of a competitor, further investigations of Microsoft for "suspected abuse of dominant market position."[70]

Earlier, the EU had challenged and disapproved the proposed General Electric/Honeywell merger,[71] which had been approved by the U.S. authorities. While EU disapproval did not, technically, prevent the merger, it was likely a prominent factor in the decision of those companies not to consummate the merger as it would have prevented the merged entity from doing business within the EU.

Some observers, therefore, have questioned whether the EU has been using its antitrust laws and policies to protect its businesses from U.S. competition.[72] Alternatively, given that the complaints about dominant firm behavior or opposition to proposed mergers often have come from U.S. companies that (would) compete with those dominant or merged firms, other observers have accused the complaining firms of jurisdiction-shopping when they fail to get the relief they seek from U.S. antitrust agencies or U.S. courts.[73] A third set of observers argues that antitrust enforcement has been minimal in the United States and therefore the EU is playing an essential role in protecting consumers and actual and potential competition.[74]

Commentators have identified two factors that may explain why competition law has developed differently in the United States and the EU.

First, until recently, many sectors in the European economy were characterized by large government- owned monopolies and as those entities have moved toward privatization and competitive entry has been allowed, there has been concern that those dominant incumbent firms could exploit their positions to limit the effectiveness of competition. Thus, EU competition policy has focused on protecting the market mechanism from practices that might not be viewed as illegal in the United States because they might not have an impact on consumers. From this perspective, it is historical coincidence that more stringent EU laws are being applied to dominant U.S. firms. In contrast, although there were government-sanctioned monopolies in the United States – notably in telecommunications and electricity markets – the firms in those industries were not government entities and comprised a much smaller portion of the overall economy than did their EU counterparts. Thus, antitrust law, policy, and enforcement have been less concerned about protecting market mechanisms, which are viewed as robust.[75]

Second, the U.S. antitrust agencies and the courts may have been concerned that markets have been distorted by the high cost of antitrust litigation, with resulting losses in efficiency, due to certain features that have not been adopted in Europe – e.g., private enforcement of the antitrust laws, class action law suits, extensive rights to discovery, and lay juries. They therefore may have preferred policies that constrain litigation. To this end, the U.S. agencies and courts have chosen to carve out "safe harbors" for certain activities where the dominant firm may in fact be exploiting its monopoly position but where it would be difficult to demonstrate consumer harm.[76] These are the same activities that often are successfully challenged in the EU – e.g., loyalty rebates, bundled discounts, exclusive dealing, tying arrangements, refusals to deal or license.

PROSPECTS[77]

On balance, U.S.-EU commercial relations are healthy and mutually advantageous. While the future course of the relationship is difficult to predict, there are major forces both for cooperation and conflict that will have an important bearing on the direction of the relationship. The most salient of these considerations are presented below.

Forces for Cooperation

The forces for cooperation are both economic and political. Three important factors are integration of markets, institutional arrangements, and a shared interest in maintaining and advancing the multilateral world trading system.

Integration of Markets

The sheer size and importance of commercial ties is a key force for cooperation. A growing number of companies in both the United States and Europe view the size, dynamism, and relative openness of each other's markets as critical to their commercial success. From the U.S. perspective, the EU market is increasingly open, standardized and growing. From the EU perspective, the U.S . remains the largest open market in the world. The six to seven million jobs on both sides of the Atlantic dependent on tightly integrated markets give rise to strong and politically active interest groups that lobby in favor of maintaining friendly bilateral ties, reducing regulations, and in opposing protectionist proposals.

The high level of integration of markets, both in goods and capital, is accompanied by heated competition for market share. Market forces and competition are driving economic convergence in a number of policy areas, such as financial services and antitrust enforcement. In the process, some trade friction and the need for policy intervention may be avoided.

In the few cases where trade disputes have led to retaliation, the high degree of market integration has served as a fire-wall or buffer, insuring that retaliation does not become excessive. Due to the high degree of cross-investments and intra-industry trade, retaliation affecting the largest sectors of U.S.-EU trade (i.e. machinery, electrical machinery, optical equipment, aircraft, vehicles, organic chemicals, and pharmaceuticals) is highly unlikely. This is because many of the products in these sectors are used in the production process by the other side. Thus, it becomes impossible to hurt the other without disrupting one's own producer interests and thousands of jobs on both sides of the Atlantic.

Institutional Arrangements

Various institutions and annual high-level meetings are also working to keep the relationship on an even keel. Beginning in the 1990s, the U.S. and EU agreed to an expanded range of dialogue and cooperation. Under the 1995 New Transatlantic Agenda (NTA), both sides tried to make progress on a positive economic agenda achievable in the short run. The NTA has been followed by a number of other specific bilateral initiatives designed to tackle remaining barriers, many of which involve regulation rather than traditional tariffs or quotas. The Transatlantic Economic Council (TEC) is the most recent institution established to reinvigorate efforts to resolve remaining disputes and to deepen the level of economic integration. Whether the TEC will prove a more successful entity for reducing remaining transatlantic regulatory and non-tariff barriers to trade remains uncertain.

There appears to be little support, however, for any big new policy initiative such as a Transatlantic Free Trade Area. This may be due, in large part, to continuing differences over agricultural policy. In the past, such initiatives have been proposed by those who hoped that U.S.-EU political relations could be bolstered by a grander economic foundation.

Shared Interest

The two sides share an important interest in promoting an open, stable, and multilateral world trading system. Both partners have placed a high priority on bringing the long-running Doha Round of multilateral trade negotiations to a successful conclusion. While U.S.-EU differences over agricultural policies continue to affect their ability to exert joint leadership, resistance on the part of key developing countries, such as India and Brazil, to a comprehensive Doha Round package of concessions has been a formidable reason for the continuing stalemate.

Given quite similar interests in bolstering the multilateral trading system, many analysts say that both sides could cooperate more in addressing the rising economic challenge posed by China. Specifically, they could work together to persuade China to abide by its WTO commitments, as well as to pressure China to let the value of its currency be determined by market forces. Cooperation of this kind could not only support U.S. and EU multilateral trade interests, but also promote stronger bilateral ties.

Forces for Conflict

While the United States and EU cooperate in a range of areas to the benefit of both sides, differences and disputes often attract more press coverage. The intractable nature of some disputes embedded in regulatory barriers, differences over the use of the WTO dispute settlement system, and rivalry could mean that conflict and tensions remain a seemingly durable feature of the relationship.

Intractable Problems

A number of U.S.-EU trade disputes have focused increasingly on differences in regulation, rather than traditional barriers such as tariffs or subsidies. Regulatory requirements established primarily with domestic consumer and environmental protection or public health concerns in mind are not designed to discriminate between domestic and imported goods and services. But they may have the secondary effect of distorting or discriminating against the free flow of international trade, which, in turn, could lead to disputes. For this reason, transatlantic regulatory disputes over beef hormones and genetically modified foods can be more bitter and difficult to resolve than traditional trade disputes, in so far as both sides feel their actions are justified by democratically derived decisions.

There have been specific challenges raised by the application of modern biotechnology to food production. The Uruguay Round Sanitary and Phytosanitary Standards (SPS) Agreement was designed to deal with this issue. It requires countries that impose regulations or trade bans to protect the health of plants, animals, and people to base such decisions on risk assessments derived from scientific evidence.[78] But the SPS requirement of a sound scientific basis is open to varying interpretations.

Ambiguities in the SPS agreement are complicated because many European consumers believe that avoidance of production practices associated with biotechnology is a value in itself. For these consumers, scientific studies showing that such technologies do not result in threats to human or animal health may not be convincing. Given these strong views, many European officials want leeway to impose trade restrictions on a "precautionary basis" and others want to renegotiate the SPS agreement. Both avenues could open up a large loophole for discriminatory trade barriers.

Even if these conflicts are not primarily due to the deliberate use of health, safety, or environmental standards as trade barriers, mistrust grows in terms of how much effort government authorities may have put into managing public concerns through educational efforts. Under these circumstances, disputes resulting from such differences are unlikely to be resolved; at best they may be contained.

WTO Differences

The United States and EU are the most active participants in the WTO Dispute Settlement System, both as petitioning and defending parties. U.S. cases against the EU tend to revolve around closure of markets to U.S. exporters or the adverse impact of state intervention or aid on U.S. sales in third markets. Cases involving beef hormones and GMOs fall in the first category and Boeing's complaint against Airbus in the latter category. EU complaints against the U.S., on the other hand, tend to involve more technical concerns about U.S. trade or tax law that are inconsistent with WTO obligations and that may confer indirect advantages for U.S. firms.

These varied approaches, which have caused considerable transatlantic tension, particularly in the case of the EU's challenge to U.S. tax benefits for exporters, have their roots in very different institutional arrangements. On the U.S. side, private sector concerns are formally considered in the trade policy making process. As a result, denial of market access opportunities is a priority concern for U.S. trade policymakers. On the other hand, some observers maintain that the EU often uses trade for foreign policy purposes by challenging the United States on a wide range of mostly technical issues. Not only does this approach allegedly help bolster the European Commission's role vis-a-vis member states as the protector of EU interests, but also promotes its image as a leading defender of rule-based multilateralism and global governance.[79]

Rivalry

A straightforward explanation for many transatlantic trade disputes may be that the U.S. and EU both aspire to lead in setting rules for global trade and investment, including environmental and safety rules that impinge on trade. The United States may think its rules should prevail given the historically dominant role of the U.S. economy. The EU is itself a system of market liberalization, and it could use trade to spread its own model of regulation and market integration to the rest of the world. If successful, European rules on regulations affecting health and safety, competition policy, government procurement, and investment will shape future parameters of trade liberalization. Beyond indirectly challenging the United States for global trade leadership, this process of spreading rules and regulations for trade may also be intended to facilitate commercial success for European companies.[80]

There is also a concern that competition between the United States and the EU to secure bilateral and regional trade agreements could have negative consequences for the world trading system. The efforts of both sides to cut deals bilaterally and regionally is a form of normal commercial rivalry between two superpowers for markets, jobs, and profits. However, some analysts worry that that such competition could foster a form of rival regionalism that undercuts the multilateral trading system on which both depend.

End Notes

[1] This section was written by Raymond J. Ahearn, Specialist in International Trade and Finance, Foreign Affairs, Defense, and Trade Division.

[2] This section was written by Raymond J. Ahearn, Specialist in International Trade and Finance, Foreign Affairs, Defense, and Trade Division.

[3] For basic background information of the EU, see CRS Report RS2 1372, *The European Union: Questions and Answers,* by Kristin Archick. The members of the EU are as follows: Austria, Belgium, Bulgaria, Cyprus, the Czech Republic, Denmark, Estonia, Finland, France, Germany, Greece, Hungary, Ireland, Italy, Latvia, Lithuania, Luxembourg, Malta, the Netherlands, Poland, Portugal, Romania, Slovakia, Slovenia, Spain, Sweden, and the United Kingdom. For a comprehensive treatment of the EU, see *Demystifying the European Union: The Enduring Logic of Regional Integration*, Lanham: Rowman & Littlefield, 2007, by Roy H. Ginsberg.

[4] This has included cooperation in completing many different multilateral trade liberalization rounds under the auspices of the General Agreement on Tariffs and Trade (GATT).

[5] International Monetary Fund, *Global Financial Stability,* September 2007.

[6] International Monetary Fund, *Directions of Trade Statistics Yearbook: 2007.*

[7] *Global Financial Stability Report,* International Monetary Fund, September 2007, Statistical Appendix, Table 3.

[8] For more data and analysis, see CRS Report RL30608, *EU-U.S. Economic Ties: Framework, Scope, and Magnitude*, by William H. Cooper.

[9] U.S. Census Bureau Foreign Trade Statistics. In 2006, Germany ranked #5, the United Kingdom #6, France, #8, the Netherlands #11, and Italy #14.

[10] The fact that the EU share of the U.S. global trade deficit declined from 18% in 2002 and 2003 to 14% in both 2006 and 2007 is a further reflection of the impact that exchange rate changes are having on trade flows.

[11] *The Economist,* "Love the one you're with; Exchange rates," October 20, 2007.

[12] Position Paper on a Transatlantic Framework Agreement, Business Europe, March 1, 2007.

[13] To chair the TEC, the U.S. side named Alan Hubbard, Assistant to the President for Economic Policy and Director of the National Economic Council, and the EU appointed Gunter Verheugen, Vice President of the European Commission and Commissioner for Enterprise and Industry.

[14] For more information on the TEC, see Section IV in the U.S.-EU Framework for Advancing Transatlantic Economic Integration, April 2007, available at [http://www.whitehouse.gov/news/releases/2007/04/20070430-4.html].

[15] The European Commission serves as a kind of executive branch for the EU. The EU is the legal entity with competence in the international trade and economic realm.

[16] *Inside U.S. Trade,* "Trans-Atlantic Talks on Harmonizing Rules to Ensure Transparency, OMB's Dudly Says," December 6, 2007.

[17] *Inside U.S. Trade,* "TEC Highlights EU Poultry Ban Resolution Next Year," November 16, 2007.

[18] This section was written by Raymond J. Ahearn, Specialist in International Trade and Finance, Foreign Affairs, Defense, and Trade Division.

[19] CRS calculations based on data from Global Trade Atlas.

[20] CRS Report RL33944, *Trade Primer: Qs and As on Trade Concepts, Performance, and Policy*, by Raymond J Ahearn, et. al., pp. 4-5.

[21] European Commission, United States Barriers to Trade and Investment, February 2007, and 2007 National Trade Estimate Report on Foreign Trade Barriers, Office of the United States Trade Representative.

[22] This section was written by John W. Fischer, Specialist in Transportation Policy, Resources, Science, and Industry Division.

[23] USTR National Trade Estimates Report: 2000, pp. 102-104.

[24] Burger, Bettina. "Transatlantic Economic Relations: Common Interests and Conflicts in High Technology and Industrial Policies," In *Transatlantic Relations in A Global Economy*, p. 110.

[25] *Inside U.S. Trade*, "WTO Boeing Panel Probes U.S. on NASA Contracts, State Taxwes," February 1, 2008.

[26] [http://www.speednews.com/speednews_files/data/249.pdf]

[27] Boeing has rethought its position on the large aircraft market. On November 14, 2005 Boeing launched the 747-8, a new stretched derivative of the venerable 747. Boeing had 103 orders for the aircraft by year end 2007, many of which are for a freighter configuration of the aircraft.

[28] For discussion of this contract, see CRS Report RL34398, *Air Force Air Refueling: The KC-X Acquisition Program*, by William Knight and Christopher Bolkcom.

[29] This section was written by Charles E. Hanrahan, Senior Specialist in Agricultural Policy, Resources, Science, and Industry Division.

[30] "Final Report Upholds Sanctions in U.S.-EU WTO Hormone Case", *Inside U.S. Trade*, January 11, 2008, viewed at [http://www.insidetrade.com/secure/dsply_nl_txt .asp?f=wto2002.ask&dh=101359414&q=]. The preliminary panel report is discussed in "Interim Ruling Faults EU Hormone Ban, U.S., Canada Sanctions", *Inside U.S. Trade*, August 17, 2007, viewed at [http://www.insidetrade.com/secure/dsply _nl_txt.asp?f=wto2002.ask&dh=8835467 1 &q=hormones].

[31] USTR, January 14, 2008, "Statement on EC-Biotech Dispute" viewed at [http://www.ustr.gov/Document_Library/Press_Releases/2008/January/Statement_on_E C-Biotech_Dispute.html]

[32] This section was written by Raymond J. Ahearn, Specialist in International Trade and Finance, Foreign Affairs, Defense, and Trade Division.

[33] For U.S. data, see Coalition of Service Industries Research and Education Foundation Report, *Services Drive U.S. Growth and Jobs: The Importance of Services by State and Congressional District*, June 2007.

[34] Survey of Current Business, October 2007 edition.

[35] This section was written by John W. Fischer, Specialist in Transportation Policy, Resources, Science and Industry Division.

[36] Flottau, Jens. "Cloudy Skies: This Year's Version of U.S./EU Open Skies Draws Mixed Responses Throughout Europe," *Aviation Week*, March 12, 2007.

[37] "Airlines, Pilot Group Lukewarm on First Stage of U.S.-EU Deal" *Aviation Daily*, December 3, 2007. p. 3.

[38] European Parliament, *Committee on Transport and Tourism*, Draft Legislative Resolution on the EU-US aviation agreement. 2006/0058 (CNS), July 30, 2007.

[39] Clark, Nocola. "U.S. Aims to Ease EU Concern On Aviation Bill," *The International Herald Tribune*, July 18, 2007, p. 10.

[40] This section was written by Walter W. Eubanks, Specialist in Financial Institutions, Government and Finance Division.

[41] European Commission, "Nine months left to deliver the FSAP," *Eighth Progress Report on the FSAP*, June 3, 2003, p. 14.

[42] Steve Burkholder, "Politics of Global Accounting Efforts Take Center Stage at Convergence Conference,"*BNA Banking Report*, October 8, 2007, p. 2.

[43] For more information on developments the implementation of the MiFID, See the [http://ec.europa.eu/internal_market/securities/news_en.htm],visited January 15, 2008.

[44] Joe Kirwin, "Selby Warns Subprime Collapse Fallout will Worsen as Union Slams Commissioner," *BNA Banking Report*, August 27, 2007.

[45] This section was written by Raymond J. Ahearn, Specialist in International Trade and Finance, Foreign Affairs, Defense, and Trade Division.

[46] Center for Transatlantic Relations, Johns Hopkins University, *The Transatlantic Economy 2008, Executive Summary*, by Daniel S. Hamilton and Joseph P. Quinlan. Available at [http://transatlantic.sais-jhu.edu]

[47] Ibid.

[48] This section was written by Charles B. Goldfarb, Specialist in Telecommunications Policy, Resources, Science, and Industry Division, and Janice E. Rubin, Legislative Attorney, American Law Division.

[49] *See, for example*, Randolph W. Tritell, "International Antitrust Convergence: A Positive View," 19 Antitrust 25 (Summer 2005). The United States seeks convergence, rather than harmonization, of antitrust policy because harmonization implies uniformity of legal provisions or their application, which would be impractical given the variation across jurisdictions in levels of economic development, legal systems, histories, and cultures.

[50] *See, for example*, Margaret Bloom, "The U.S. and EU Move Towards Substantial Antitrust Convergence on Consumer Welfare Based Enforcement," 19 Antitrust 18 (Summer 2005); Tritell, *supra*, note 49; Ronald W. Davis and Jennifer M. Driscoll, "The Urge to Converge – The New EU Discussion Paper on Abuse of a Dominant Position," 20 Antitrust 82 (Spring 2006); Eleanor M. Fox, "What is Harm to Competition? Exclusion Practices and Anticompetitive Effect," 70 Antitrust Law Journal 371 (2002); Eleanor M. Fox, "Monopolization, Abuse of Dominance, and the Indeterminacy of Economics: The U.S./E.U. Divide," Utah Law Review 725 (2006); John Vickers, "Competition Law and Economics: a Mid-Atlantic Viewpoint," 3 European Competition Law Journal 1 (2007); J. Thomas Rosch, Commissioner Federal Trade Commission, "Has the Pendulum Swung Too Far: Some Reflections on U.S. and EC Jurisprudence," based on remarks presented at the Bates White Fourth Annual Antitrust Conference (Washington, D.C., June 25, 2007); J. Thomas Rosch, Commissioner, Federal Trade Commission, "I Say Monopoly, You Say Dominance: The Continuing Divide on the Treatment of Dominant Firms, Is it the Economics?," presentation at the International Bar Association, Antitrust Section Conference (Florence, Italy, September 8, 2007); Thomas O. Barnett, Assistant Attorney General, Antitrust Division, U.S. Department of Justice, "Global Antitrust Enforcement," presented at the Georgetown Law Global Antitrust Enforcement Symposium (Washington, D.C., September 26, 2007); Thomas O. Barnett, Assistant Attorney General, Antitrust Division, U.S. Department of Justice, "The Gates of Creative Destruction: The Need for Clear and Objective Standards for Enforcing Section 2 of the Sherman Act," opening remarks for the Antitrust Division and Federal Trade Commission Hearings Regarding Section 2 of the Sherman Act (Washington, D.C., June 20, 2006), at 9-10; J. Bruce McDonald, Deputy Assistant Attorney General, Antitrust Division, U.S. Department of Justice, "Section 2 and Article 82: Cowboys and Gentlemen," remarks presented to the Second Annual Conference of the College of Europe (Brussels, June 16-17, 2005).

[51] *See, for example*, Bloom, *supra*, note 50; and Rosch,"I Say Monopoly ...,"*supra*, note 50.

[52] For a more detailed discussion of U.S. law on monopolization, see CRS Report RL33708, *The Distinction Between Monopoly and Monopolization in Antitrust Law*, by Janice E. Rubin.

[53] *See, e.g.*, United States v. E.I. duPont de Nemours & Co., 351 U.S. 377, 39 1-92 (1956).

[54] *See* McDonald, *supra*, note 50.

[55] Anheuser-Busch, Inc. v. G.T. Britts Distributing, Inc., 44 F.Supp. 2d, 172, 174 (N.D.N.Y. 1999), *quoting* George Haug Co. v. Rolls Royce Motor Cars, Inc., 148 F.3d 136, 139 (2d Cir. 1998), which *quoted* Capitol Imaging v. Mohawk Valley Med. Assocs., 996 F2d 537, 543 (2d Cir. 1993), *cert. denied*, 510 U.S. 947 (1993).

[56] Wichita Clinic, P.A. v. Columbia/HCA Healthcare Corp., 45 F.Supp. 2d 1164, 1193 (D. Kansas 1999), *quoting* Brooke Group v. Brown & Williamson Tobacco, 509 U.S. 209, 224 (1993), *quoting* Brown Shoe v. United States, 370 U.S. 294, 320 (1962 (emphasis in Brown Shoe).

[57] *See, for example*, Thomas O. Barnett, Assistant Attorney General, Antitrust Division, U.S. Department of Justice, "Competition Law and Policy Modernization: Lessons from the U.S. Common-Law Experience," presentation to the Lisbon Conference on Competition Law and Economics, Lisbon, Portugal, November 16, 2007.

[58] *See, for example*, Rosch, "Has the Pendulum Swung Too Far: ...," *supra*, note 50.

[59] Fox, *supra*, note 50.

[60] Emphasis added. Excerpted from "CONSOLIDATED VERSION OF THE TREATY ESTABLISHING THE EUROPEAN COMMUNITY," as that document appears on the EU web site, [http: //eur-lex.europa. eu/en/treaties 1 2002E/htm/C_20023 25EN .00330 1 .html#anArt82], viewed on January 28, 2008.

[61] *See, for example*, Rosch, "I Say Monopoly ...," *supra*, note 50. The post-Chicago School models also tend to focus on consumer surplus and not include in consumer welfare the producer surplus that a dominant firm may capture from its actions.

[62] Fox, *supra*, note 50.

[63] *Id.*

[64] *See, for example*, Davis and Driscoll, *supra*, note 50.

[65] *See, e.g.*, Philip Lowe, Director General, Directorate General for Competition, European Commission, "Remarks on Unilateral Conduct," Speech before a session of the Federal Trade Commission and Antitrust Division Hearings on Section 2 of the Sherman Act (Washington, D.C., September 11, 2006); McDonald, *supra*, note 50.

[66] *E.g.*, Spectrum Sports, Inc. v. McQuillan 506 U.S. 447, 458 (1993): "The purpose of the [Sherman] Act is not to protect businesses from the working of the market; it is to protect the public from the failure of the market. The law directs itself not against conduct which is competitive, even severely so, but against conduct which unfairly tends to destroy competition itself. It does so not out of solicitude for private concerns but out of concern for the public interest." *See, also*, Brunswick Corp. v. Pueblo Bowl-O-Mat, Inc., 429 U.S. 477, 488 (1977); Cargill, Inc. v. Monfort of Colorado, Inc., 479 U.S. 104, 116-117(1986); Brown Shoe Co. v. United States, 370 U.S. 294, 320 (1962).

[67] For a more thorough treatment of the difference in emphasis, *see* McDonald, *supra*, note 50.

[68] Commission Decision in Case COMP/C-3/37.792 Microsoft (2004); Microsoft Corp. v. Commission of the European Communities, No. T-20 1/4 (EU Ct. 1st Inst. 2007).

[69] 87 F.Supp. 2d 30 (D.D.C. 2000) ("Conclusions of Law"); 97 F.Supp. 2d 59 (D.D.C. 2000) ("Final Judgment"); *aff'd in part, rev. in part,* "Final Judgment" *vacated, remanded to be assigned to new judge*, 253 F.3d 34 (D.C. Cir. 2001); *cert. den.*, 534 U.S. 952 (2001); *on remand*, 231 F.Supp.2d 144 (D.D.C. 2002); *aff'd sub nom.*, Massachusetts v. Microsoft Corp., 373 F.3d 1199 (D.C.Cir. 2004).

[70] EU Press Release re MEMO/08/19 (Brussels, 1/14/2008).

[71] The Competition Commission's decision was rendered in July 2001, and affirmed by the Court of First Instance in December 2005 (General Electric Co. v. Commission of European Communities, Case No. T-2 10/01, Honeywell v. Commission of European Communities, Case No. T-209/01 (CFI 2005).

[72] *See, for example*, "FreedomWorks, Dick Armey Criticize European Ruling Against Microsoft,"September 17, 2007, available at [http://www.freedomworks.org/newsroom /press_template.php?press_id=23 14], viewed on January 7, 2008.

[73] *See, for example,* Scott M. Fulton, III, "US Antitrust Chief, EU Competition Chief Spar Over Microsoft," *betanews   at   CES   '08,*   September   20,   2007,   available   at [http://www.betanews.com/article/US-Antitrust_Chief_EU_Competition_Chief_Spar_Over_Microsoft/1 19029934], viewed on January 7, 2008.

[74] *See, for example,* American Antitrust Institute, "Microsoft, the European Union, and the United States: A Statement by the AAI," September 24, 2007, available at [http://www.antitrustinstitute. org/Archives/miceu3.ashx], viewed on January 28, 2008. Representatives of the U.S. and EU competition agencies, however, have continued to stress their close working relationship despite their sometimes high-profile disagreements. *See, e.g.,* "U.S., EU Enforcers Concede Differences, Stress Necessity for Continued Cooperation," 81 Antitrust & Trade Regulation Report 462 (11/23/2001).

[75] Congress passed legislation to guide the transition from monopoly to competition in those markets, imposing certain requirements on the incumbent firms that were intended to foster competitive entry. For example, the Telecommunications Act of 1996 (P.L. 104-104) imposed certain requirements on the Bell Operating Companies to provide new entrants access to their networks during the transition. The U.S. Supreme Court ruled, in a private antitrust challenge, that violation of the act's requirements by an incumbent telecommunications firm did not also constitute an antitrust violation since those regulatory requirements exceeded those of the antitrust laws. (*Verizon Communications, Inc. v. Law Offices of Curtis V. Trinko*, 540 U.S. 398 (2004)) For a detailed discussion of the *Trinko* decision, *see* CRS Report RS21723, *Verizon Communications, Inc. v. Trinko: Telecommunications Consumers Cannot Use Antitrust Laws to Remedy Access Violations of Telecommunications Law,* by Janice E. Rubin.

[76] *See, for example,* Barnett, "The Gates of Creative Destruction: ...," *supra,* note 50.

[77] This section was written by Raymond J. Ahearn, Specialist in International Trade and Finance, Foreign Affairs, Defense, and Trade Division.

[78] A related multilateral code, the Agreement on Technical Barriers to Trade (TBT), covers other types of regulations such as labeling and packaging.

[79] John Van Oudenaren, *Uniting Europe,* Rowman & Littlefield Publishers, 2005, p. 376.

[80] Sophie Meunier and Kalypso Nicolaidis, "The European Union as a conflicted trade power," *Journal of European Public Policy,* 13:6 September 2006: p. 912; and Bruce Stokes, "Bilateralism Trumps Multilateralism," *National Journal,* December 16, 2006.

[80] Sophie Meunier and Kalypso Nicolaidis, "The European Union as a conflicted trade power," Journal of European Public Policy, 13:6 September 2006: p. 912; and Bruce Stokes, "Bilateralism Trumps Multilateralism," National Journal, December 16, 2006.

In: European Union - U.S. Trade and Investment... ISBN: 978-1-60741-886-3
Editors: Linus R. Wilkens pp.63-70   © 2010 Nova Science Publishers, Inc.

Chapter 4

EUROPE'S NEW TRADE AGENDA

Raymond J. Ahearn

SUMMARY

Soon after the Doha Round of multilateral trade negotiations came to a standstill in July 2006, the European Union (EU) announced its intention to enter into more bilateral and regional free trade agreements (FTAs). While the EU historically has been a leading force for preferential trade agreements, its main priority from 2001-2006 was negotiating an ambitious Doha Round agreement. Given that the EU is a global economic superpower, its resumption of a bilateral and preferential trade strategy has implications for the global trading system, as well as for U.S. trade interests. As articulated in an October 2006 report, the EU will prioritize FTAs with regions and countries according to their economic potential rather than on development aims. The July 2008 breakdown of the Doha negotiations may reinforce this approach. This chapter summarizes the EU's new initiative, casts the initiative in historical perspective, and assesses the implications of this shift for the global trading system and for U.S. interests.

THE EU'S TRADE SHIFT

The European Commission announced on October 4, 2006, that it was adopting a new trade policy that will support efforts to foster economic growth and create jobs. Based on concern that European exports have not been successful enough in some of the most rapidly growing economies in the world, the Commission proposed shifting EU trade policy from sole reliance on multilateral trade negotiations to proposing a new generation of bilateral and regional FTAs.[1]

The essence of the strategy will be that FTAs should be negotiated with the EU's most important trading partners around the globe, as soon as possible. Whereas previous attempts to secure FTAs were predicated on promoting development or boosting regional co-operation, the new strategy now will be based on market potential (economic size and growth) and the level of protection against EU exports.

Based on mostly economic criteria, the Commission identified South Korea, India, and ASEAN as priority negotiating partners. These three trading partners combine high levels of protection with large market potential and they are active in concluding FTAs with EU competitors. The Commission hopes to negotiate an FTA with South Korea in one year and to reach accords with India and ASEAN within two years.[2] The Commission also has identified Mercosur (Brazil, Argentina, Paraguay, and Uruguay), Russia, and the Gulf Cooperation Council as the next tier of candidates because they combine market potential and fairly high levels of protection. According to the Commission, China also meets many of these criteria, but requires special attention.

In terms of content, the Commission states that the new FTAs would need to be comprehensive and ambitious in coverage, aiming at the highest possible degree of trade liberalization. The FTAs would also need to include such issue areas as services, investment, intellectual property rights, public procurement, and competition policy.

Finally, the Commission maintains that any decision to launch an FTA negotiation would not only be based on economic criteria, but also broader political considerations. This is because FTAs are viewed by the Commission as an integral part of the EU's bilateral relations with the country or region concerned.

EVOLUTION OF EU TRADE POLICY

Historically, the EU was an early, major promoter of preferential trade agreements.[3] In the 1960s, it concluded the Yaounde Agreements, then reciprocal, with former colonies. This was followed in 1975 by the Lome Treaties, giving easy, often free non- reciprocal access for the mostly African former colonies to the European Community (EC). In the 1970s, a series of preferential, non-reciprocal agreements were signed with Mediterranean countries such as Turkey and Greece — and bilateral FTAs in industrial goods with the then six European Free Trade Association (EFTA) countries. Existing overseas territories had yet another special regime, and the EC generalized system of preferences was initiated in 1971, creating what was dubbed a "pyramid of preferences."[4]

A second wave of regionalism began in the late 1980s. After the Berlin Wall fell, the EU concluded Association Agreements with 10 countries in Central and Eastern Europe and Trade and Cooperation Agreements with all of the Commonwealth of Independent States (comprised of most of the former Soviet Union states). Other major initiatives, including FTAs with South Africa and Mexico, followed suit and by 1999 total trade between countries with which the EU has free trade and preferential agreements (including intra-EU trade) was over three times U.S. trade with its free trade agreement partners.[5]

Beginning in the mid-1990s, the EU began to give priority to the multilateralism of the WTO over bilateral agreements for a number of reasons. Most generally, Brussels saw multilateralism and the WTO as a mechanism for managing globalization. By using the single European market as a model for its global trade liberalization agenda, European policymakers hoped to control globalization more tightly. The steps involved in managing globalization in trade included widening the definition of trade issues subject to new issues such as investment, services, intellectual property rights, and competition policy; and redistributing the benefits and costs of globalization, both outside and inside Europe.[6]

In the process, the EU put itself forward as the leading champion of the global multilateral system. While it did not abandon any of its preferential agreements, under the leadership of its Trade Commissioner Pascal Lamy, the EU in 2001 halted the negotiation of any new FTAs while Doha was underway.

Other countries, including the United States and China, however, did not follow the EU's example. Beginning with the Bush Presidency in 2002, the

United States which had shunned such arrangements for decades because it saw itself as the post-1945 champion of an open, multilateral system, began pursuing bilateral and regional FTAs with many countries around the world with much greater vigor. Under the banner of "competitive liberalization," many in the United States saw an opportunity to catch up with the EU's long record of pursuing preferential agreements.[7]

Suspension of the multilateral Doha Round of WTO talks in July 2006 prompted the EU to move rapidly back towards a strong reliance on bilateral agreements. While the stated goal is to use these trade agreements as a tool to enhance European competitiveness, a less obvious goal may now be to catch up to the United States in signing bilateral and regional trade deals, bringing about a convergence in the trade policies of the two economic superpowers.

Movement by the EU towards a reliance on bilateral agreements is seen by some as a more natural policy position. One scholar, for example, has argued that the EU has a deeply rooted tradition of negotiating bilateral preferential agreements and of using trade policy as an instrument of foreign policy. In the formulation of trade policy, this scholar maintains that the EU is an incomplete state and uses trade policy as an instrument of completeness with all the attributes of sovereignty. And since foreign relations are inherently bilateral, he argues that the use of trade policy instruments for foreign policy imparts a bilateral bias.[8]

In the context of transatlantic commercial relations, a case is sometimes made that the EU often uses trade for foreign policy purposes by challenging the United States on a wide range of mostly technical issues. Not only does this approach help bolster the Commission's role vis-a-vis member states as the protector of EU economic interests, but also promotes its image as a leading defender of rules-based multilateralism and global governance.[9]

IMPLICATIONS FOR THE GLOBAL TRADING SYSTEM

EU trade officials acknowledge the risks that a bilateral agenda could carry for the multilateral trading system by diverting and complicating trade, by eroding the principle of non-discrimination, and by excluding the weakest economies. To have a positive impact, the EU maintains that its FTAs will be comprehensive in scope, provide for liberalization of substantially all trade (as required by the WTO) and go beyond current WTO disciplines. EU trade officials maintain that any new FTAs will be WTO-plus, which provides either wider or deeper obligations than currently exist.[10]

How likely, one can ask, might the EU's potential FTAs be WTO-plus and serve to liberalize as well as simplify the world trading system? If history is any guide, the answer may not be encouraging. Similarly, an analysis of the current hurdles posed in negotiating deep FTAs across a full range of sectors casts a skeptical light over the EU's claim that its bilateral agenda will likely become a building block, not a stumbling block, for multilateral liberalization.

In the long history of EU preferential agreements, there has been no such thing as a standard trade agreement. According to one study, agreements usually cover most or all industrial goods, but liberalization is sometimes asymmetric and transition periods differ. In agriculture, market access to the EU tends to be product specific, selective, and rarely without any form of restriction. And the huge variety of preferential agreements tend to create a confusing array of rules of origin that make trade more complicated and costly.[11]

During 2007 there was much criticism from some member states and NGOs of the Commission's efforts to negotiate Economic Partnership Agreements (EPAs) with African, Caribbean and Pacific (ACP) developing countries. These agreements were being negotiated to supplant one-way preferences that expired on January 1, 2008. Most of the ACP countries resisted signing new Economic Partnership Agreements (EPAs) proposed by the EU on the grounds that they contained the worst and most unfair elements of what was on the table in the Doha Round. Specifically, many of these countries felt they were being being forced to open their markets to subsidized European agricultural products or to negotiate on issues they do not want to discuss. As a result, negotiations on full EPAs continue this year.[12]

Are any of the EU's prospective FTAs likely to buck these trends by achieving comprehensive coverage and reciprocal liberalization or market openings in sensitive sectors? While it is impossible to predict with a high degree of assurance, a reason for a pessimistic view is that there are continuing strong political pressures to insulate European agricultural producers against liberalization. Efforts, for example, to reach an FTA with Mercosur have been on and off for nearly a decade due in part to EU reluctance to offer greater concessions on agricultural trade barriers (particularly sugar and beef).[13]

In the view of one analyst, "any FTA that the EU signs with the big boys, such as India and China, is likely to be quick and dirty and fairly trade-light." Furthermore, he points out that both India and China's existing FTAs with other countries are "narrow and shallow," excluding many goods and sectors from cuts in protective tariffs, prompting scepticism that they will be eager to enter into deep comprehensive agreements.[14]

This is not to suggest that the EU is ever likely to abandon its commitment to an open multilateral system. Regional blocs would be opposed by EU multinationals because they would lose far more from developments that threatened their access to global markets than they might gain from the protections that a regional bloc would offer. But at the same time, the EU faces formidable obstacles in achieving its stated goal of driving the global trading system forward if it ends up negotiating weak and partial FTAs.[15]

IMPLICATIONS FOR U.S. INTERESTS

The EU's activist, bilateral market opening trade agenda is remarkably similar to the Bush Administration's agenda. Both economic superpowers assert that the ambitious bilateral agreements they seek to negotiate will serve to drive global liberalization forward in areas such as investment, competition, and public procurement where WTO rules do not yet fully apply. They both maintain that carefully constructed and comprehensive bilateral agreements with chosen partners can create new trade as well as new jobs for their most competitive companies. And for both Brussels and Washington, the choice of negotiating partners is based not only on market potential, but also on broader political considerations.

While some may argue the United States, thus, is not in any position to complain about the thrust of the EU bilateral initiative, the content of any of the EU's bilateral or regional agreements reached could be a different matter. Both comprehensive and shallow agreements may create their own set of challenges for U.S. interests.

Comprehensive agreements, on balance, are likely to promote greater openness and create more trade than they divert. The EU maintains that it is committed to negotiating comprehensive and balanced agreements. This should benefit the United States as well, but they may do so in a distinctively European way. The EU is itself a system of market liberalization, and it wants to use trade to spread its own model of regulation and market integration to the rest of the world. If successful, European rules on regulations affecting health and safety, competition policy, government procurement, and investment will shape future parameters of trade liberalization. Beyond indirectly challenging the United States for global trade leadership, this process of spreading rules and regulations for trade may also be intended to facilitate commercial success for European companies.[16]

Shallow agreements, on the other hand, could lead to different kinds of tensions and rivalry. Hypothetically, if the EU negotiated a narrow deal with say South Korea (after the U.S. failed to implement a comprehensive agreement), it could raise suspicions in Washington that the EU action was driven as much by an effort to gain some kind of geostrategic advantage as a commercial edge. There is the possibility, in turn, that shallow agreements negotiated by the EU might prompt Washington to move in that direction as well with the two powers striving to outbid each other for FTA partners.

Competition between the United States and the EU to secure bilateral and regional trade agreements could be expected to promote normal commercial rivalry between the two superpowers for markets, jobs, and profits. Whether such competition leads to a form of rival regionalism between the United States and the EU remains unpredictable.

But the EU's more activist bilateral agenda might be a consideration in any congressional debate in 2008 or 2009 on the renewal of Trade Promotion Authority. Some Members of Congress may ask what impact the EU's new trade policy is likely to have on U.S. interests, particularly if the United States is not negotiating similar agreements. On the one hand, there may be concern that U.S. non-participation in FTA negotiations could affect Washington's ability to influence the international trade agenda, as well as put some U.S. exporters at a competitive disadvantage. On the other hand, U.S. efforts and even competition with the EU to craft new FTAs could be viewed as counterproductive to the goal of strengthening the multilateral trading system.

End Notes

[1] This section is drawn from a European Commission Staff Working Document, *Global Europe: Competing In the World* {Com(2006)567 final}, October 4, 2006.

[2] *Inside U.S. Trade*, "EU Planning Free Trade Pacts With South Korea, India, ASEAN," December 7, 2006. As of July 2008, the EU had completed 7 rounds of negotiations on a comprehensive agreement with South Korea, but little progress has been made in negotiating an FTA with India. FTA negotiations with ASEAN have not started, but remain under study.

[3] The EU, which began with the establishment of the European Economic Community (EEC), is itself a preferential trade area with an agenda of expansion. The notion that granting trade preferences to partners is the norm, rather than the exception, for the EU is supported by the fact that it conducts trade on a non-discriminatory or MFN basis with only a half dozen trading partners, including the United States and China.

[4] Jacques Pelkmans and Paul Brenton, "Bilateral Trade Agreements with the EU: Driving Forces and Effects," in *Multilateralism and Regionalism in the Post-Uruguay Round Era*, edited by Olga Memedovic, Arie Kuyenhoven, and Willem T.M. Molle, Kluwer Academic Publishers, 1999. p. 87.

[5] CRS Report RL31072, *Regional Trade Agreements: An Analysis of Trade-Related Impacts*, by Gary J. Wells.

[6] Rawi Abdeiai and Sophie Meunier, "La Règle du Jeu: France and the Paradox of Managed Globalization." Paper delivered at the 2006 Annual Meeting of the American Political Science Association, August 30-September 3, 2006, p. 9.

[7] CRS Report RL3 3463, *Trade Negotiations During the 109th Congress*, November 14, 2006, by Ian Fergusson.

[8] Patrick A. Messerlin, "MFN-Based Freer Trade and Regional Free Trade: What Role for the EU?," in *Multilateralism and Regionalism in the Post-Uruguay Round Era?* pp. 51-54.

[9] John Van Oudenaren, *Uniting Europe*, Rowman & Littlefield Publishers, 2005, p. 376.

[10] Judith Crosbie, "EU negotiates bilateral trade deals but hopes for Doha revival," *European Voice*, July 27, 2006.

[11] Pelkmans and Brenton, pp. 92-96, and Jean-Christophe Maur, "Exporting Europe's Trade Policy," *The World Economy*, November 2005, Vol. 28, pp. 1565-1590.

[12] Judith Crosbie, "Commission defends last-minute trade deals," *European Voice*, January 10, 2008.

[13] Oxford Analytica Daily Brief, "EU seeks bilateral trade deals," October 13, 2006.

[14] Razeen Sally, "What happens after the Doha Round?" *Opinion Asia*, [http://www.opinionasia.org/WhathappensafterDoha].

[15] Some critics of FTAs have argued that even if FTAs are comprehensive or "WTO-plus," the major trading powers' focus on them robs multilateral negotiations of momentum.

[16] Sophie Meunier and Kalypso Nicolaidis, "The European Union as a conflicted trade power," *Journal of European Public Policy*, 13:6 September 2006: p. 912; and Bruce Stokes, "Bilateralism Trumps Multilateralism," *National Journal*, December 16, 2006.

In: European Union - U.S. Trade and Investment... ISBN: 978-1-60741-886-3
Editors: Linus R. Wilkens pp.71-81   © 2010 Nova Science Publishers, Inc.

Chapter 5

EU-U.S. ECONOMIC TIES: FRAMEWORK, SCOPE, AND MAGNITUDE

William H. Cooper

SUMMARY

The United States and the European Union (EU) economic relationship is the largest in the world—and it is growing. The modern U.S.-European economic relationship has evolved since World War II, broadening as the six-member European Community expanded into the present 27-member European Union. The ties have also become more complex and interdependent, covering a growing number and type of trade and financial activities.

In 2007, $1,602.1 billion flowed between the United States and the EU on the current account, the most comprehensive measure of U.S. trade flows. The EU as a unit is the largest **merchandise** trading partner of the United States. In 2007, the EU accounted for $247.3 billion of total U.S. exports (or 21.3%) and for $354.7 billion of total U.S. imports (or 18.2%) for a U.S. trade deficit of $107.4 billion. The EU is also the largest U.S. trade partner when trade in **services** is added to trade in merchandise, accounting for $182.5 billion (or 38.0% of the total in U.S. services exports) and $145.8 billion (or 42.7% of total U.S. services imports) in 2007. In addition, in 2007, a net $175.5 billion *flowed* from U.S. residents to EU countries into direct investments, while a net

$148.4 billion *flowed* from EU residents to direct investments in the United States.

Policy disputes arise between the United States and the EU generating tensions which sometimes lead to bilateral trade disputes. Yet, in spite of these disputes, the U.S.-EU economic relationship remains dynamic. It is a relationship that is likely to grow in importance assuming the trends toward globalization and the enlargement of the EU continue, forcing more trade and investment barriers to fall. Economists indicate that an expanded relationship would bring economic benefits to both sides in the form of wider choices of goods and services and greater investment opportunities.

But increasing economic interdependence brings challenges as well as benefits. As the U.S. and EU economies continue to integrate, some sectors or firms will "lose out" to increased competition and will resist the forces of change. Greater economic integration also challenges long-held notions of "sovereignty," as national or regional policies have extraterritorial impact. Similarly, accepted understanding of "competition," "markets," and other economic concepts are tested as national borders dissolve with closer integration of economies.

U.S. and EU policymakers are likely to face the task of how to manage the increasingly complex bilateral economic relationship in ways that maximize benefits and keep frictions to a minimum, including developing new frameworks. For Members during the 111th Congress, it could mean weighing the benefits of greater economic integration against the costs to constituents in the context of overall U.S. national interests.

The bilateral economic relationship between the United States and the European Union (EU) is the largest such relationship in the world—and it is growing.[1] It is a relationship forged over several centuries, since the European colonization of North America.

The modern U.S.-European economic relationship has evolved since World War II. It has broadened as the six-member European Community expanded into the present 27-member European Union. The ties have also become more complex, covering a growing number and type of trade and financial activities that intertwine the economies on both sides of the Atlantic into an increasingly interdependent relationship. For Members of Congress and other policymakers, the EU remains a significant participant in the U.S. economy and a major factor in policy considerations. For example, the EU and its members are influential members of the World Trade Organization (WTO), the Organization for Economic Cooperation and Development (OECD), the International Monetary Fund (IMF) and the World Bank. These countries, together with the United States, play decisive roles in developing and implementing the missions of those institutions.

Despite the tightness of the bilateral relationship, policy tensions arise generating tensions within the relationship, sometimes leading to bilateral trade disputes.[2] The issues that arise are becoming more complex, reflecting the growing integration of the U.S. and EU economies. Yet, in spite of these disputes, the U.S.-EU economic relationship remains dynamic and one within which trillions of dollars of economic activity transpire.

This chapter provides background information and analysis of the U.S.-EU economic relationship for Members of the 111th Congress as they contemplate the costs and benefits of closer U.S. economic ties with the EU. It examines the economic and political framework of the relationship and the scope and magnitude of the ties based on data from various sources. In addition, the report analyzes the implications these factors have for U.S. economic policy toward the EU. The report will be revised as events warrant.

U.S. INTERESTS

The United States has been a strong advocate for the construction of close economic ties among the West European countries since the end of World War II. During the Cold War, the European Community served U.S. foreign policy and national security interests as a force of stability that drew former enemies—(West) Germany and France—closer together and that helped to build Western Europe into an economic bulwark against the Soviet Bloc.

The formation of an economically unified Europe has served U.S. economic interests as well by accelerating European economic growth and development which has opened trade and investment opportunities for the United States. Many studies have concluded that the formation of the EU has had a net positive economic impact on the world as a whole because it has led on balance to more trade *creation* than *diversion* of trade from other countries.

The EU continues to become a more closely knit entity with the formation of the European Monetary Union comprising 16 of the 27 members of the EU and their adoption of a common currency, the euro. These developments have already had an impact on U.S.-EU trade ties.

THE FRAMEWORK OF U.S.-EU ECONOMIC TIES

U.S.-EU economic relations exist within a framework of economic, political and security factors. Some of these factors have promoted closer economic relationships, while others have created tensions that have, at times, threatened to undermine the relationship.

The U.S.-EU economic relationship dominates the world economy by the sheer size of their combined economies. The combined population of United States and the EU members approaches 800 million people who generate a combined gross domestic product (GDP) that is roughly equivalent to 57% of world GDP in 2007.[3] Combined EU and U.S. world trade accounts for over half of all world trade. In other words, the U.S.-EU economic relationship has clout.

The United States and the EU member countries are of roughly equivalent levels of economic development and are among the most advanced in the world. As a group they include the world's wealthiest and most educated populations. The United States and the members of the EU, with a few exceptions, are major producers of advanced technologies and services. As a result U.S.-EU trade tends to be intra-industry trade; that is trade in similar products, such as cars and computers, dominate two-way trade flows. Furthermore, the United States and the EU have advanced and integrated financial sectors which facilitate large volumes of capital flows across the Atlantic. These capital flows account for a significant portion of the bilateral economic activity.

The dominance of security and defense matters is another factor influencing U.S.-EU ties. Twenty-one of the EU-27 are members of NATO, and represent an overwhelming majority of NATO's 26 members. NATO members must deal with a number of issues that pertain to foreign trade, such as defense-related government procurement, product standardization, controls of exports of dual-use technologies and related products, and economic sanctions. National security and foreign policy concerns strongly dominated the U.S.-European relationship during the Cold War.[4]

The 153-member WTO (and its predecessor, the General Agreement on Tariffs and Trade (GATT)) is a critical part of the EU-U.S. bilateral economic framework. The WTO provides the principles and rules under which the U.S. and the EU conduct much of their trade. The basic principles of most-favored-nation(MFN), or nondiscriminatory, treatment and of national treatment of imports of goods and services and of foreign investments, along with WTO rules on trade-related intellectual property rights, investment, and trade remedy practices (antidumping and countervailing duties and safeguards) are the foundation of U.S. and European trade and investment policies. The WTO also provides the mechanism by which the United States and the EU resolve many of their bilateral trade disputes.

To a lesser extent, the OECD is an important element in the U.S.-EU framework. Largely consisting of fully industrialized countries, the 30-member OECD coordinates economic policies and reviews economic conditions and polices of its members and those of some non-members. The OECD also has some rules and guidelines for trade and investment practices of its members. For example, the OECD Arrangement on Official Export Credits curbs the subsidization of exports.

EU and U.S. policies and practices form another element of the bilateral economic framework. The United States and the EU share a commitment to open trade and investment. The United States and European countries were largely instrumental in establishing the post-World War II foundation for an open international economic system. This commitment has played a large role in the strong economic ties between them. Yet, the two sides differ in some significant policy areas, for example, the EU's Common Agricultural Policy, conflicting competition policies, and the U.S. extraterritorial application of economic sanctions against Cuba and other countries. These policy differences have been a source of significant bitterness and controversy.

U.S.-EU TRADE IN GOODS AND SERVICES

The EU as a unit is the largest **merchandise** trading partner of the United States. In 2007, the EU accounted for $247.3 billion of total U.S. exports (or 21.3%) and for $54.7 billion of total U.S. imports (or 18.2%) for a U.S. trade deficit of $107.4 billion. At the same time, the United States is the largest non-EU trading partner of the EU as a whole. In 2007, EU exports to the United States accounted for 20.9% of total exports to non-EU countries, while EU imports from the United States accounted for 12.7% of total imports from non-EU countries.[5]

For a number of years, the United States realized trade surpluses with the EU. However, since 1993, the United States has been incurring growing trade deficits with the EU ($107.4 billion in 2007). Economists attribute the growth in the U.S. trade deficit with the EU to, among other factors, differences in

U.S. and economic growth rates and the weakening of the dollar compared to the euro.

Among the top U.S. exports to the EU have been aircraft, and machinery of various kinds, including computers, integrated circuits, and office machine parts. A large share of U.S. imports from the EU has consisted of passenger cars, machinery of various types, including gas turbines, computers and components, office machinery, and parts and organic chemicals. Within the EU, Germany, the United Kingdom, and France are the leading U.S. trading partners, followed by the Netherlands and Italy.

The EU is the largest U.S. trade partner when trade in **services** is added to trade in merchandise. In 2007 the EU accounted for $182.5 billion (or 38.0% of the total in U.S. services exports). Of this amount, $29.0 billion derived from receipts for various travel services, $7.5 billion from payments for passenger fares, and $17.2 billion for other transportation fees (freight and port services). Another $38.8 billion were in receipts for royalties and licensing fees and $86.7 billion derived from other private sector services, including business, professional and technical services (including legal services), and insurance. Also included under services are revenues from transfers under U.S. military contracts which equaled $3.0 billion in 2007.

In 2007, the EU accounted for $145.8 billion (or 42.7% of total U.S. services imports)—including travel services ($22.0 billion), passenger fees ($13.3 billion), and freight and port fees ($22.9 billion). Royalties and licensing fees accounted for another $11.9 billion. In addition, other private sector services accounted for $63.1 billion of imports. Also included were payments of $11.1 billion in defense-related expenditures.[6]

Table 1. U.S. Merchandise Trade with Selected Trade Partners, 2007 (billions of dollars)

Partner	U.S. Exports	U.S. Imports	U.S. Trade Turnover	U.S. Trade Balances
EU-27	247.3	354.7	602.0	-107.4
Canada	248.9	313.1	562.0	-64.2
Mexico	136.5	210.8	347.3	-74.3
China	65.3	321.5	386.8	-256.3
Japan	62.3	145.5	207.8	-82.8
World	1,163.3	1,953.6	3,116.9	-790.3

Source: U.S. Department of Commerce. Bureau of the Census.

Table 2. U.S. Trade with the European Union in Goods and Services, 1997-2007 (billions of dollars)

U.S. Exports

	1997	1998	1999	2000	2001	2002	2003	2004	2005	2006	2007
Goods & Services	240.5	232.4	236.4	257.5	244.5	238.4	250.7	283.2	314.3	353.5	424.7
Goods[a]	153.0	145.9	148.9	162.3	155.8	140.4	147.6	167.6	183.4	210.2	242.2
Services	87.5	86.5	87.6	95.2	88.7	98.0	103.2	115.6	130.8	143.3	182.5

U.S. Imports

	1997	1998	1999	2000	2001	2002	2003	2004	2005	2006	2007
Goods & Services	243.5	242.3	264.4	298.6	293.2	311.3	338.6	387.6	427.3	459.4	502.0
Goods[a]	175.8	176.1	194.5	219.9	219.5	225.4	244.9	278.9	309.0	330.4	356.2
Services	67.7	66.2	69.9	78.7	73.7	85.2	93.7	108.7	118.3	129.0	145.8

U.S. Trade Balances

	1997	1998	1999	2000	2001	2002	2003	2004	2005	2006	2007
Goods & Services	-3.0	-9.9	-28.0	-41.1	-48.7	-72.9	-87.8	-104.4	-113.0	-105.9	-77.2
Goods[a]	-22.8	-30.2	-45.6	-57.6	-63.7	-85.0	-97.3	-111.3	-125.5	-120.2	-113.9
Services	19.8	20.3	17.7	16.5	15.0	9.7	9.5	6.9	12.5	14.3	36.7

a. The figures for goods trade while essentially equivalent to those for merchandise trade in **Table 2**, are slightly lower as they are measured on a balance of payments basis, rather than a census basis.

Source: U.S. Department of Commerce. Bureau of Economic Analysis. *Survey of Current Business*. Various issues.

Table 3. U.S. Current Account Balance with EU, 2007 (billions of dollars)

Exports Goods and Services	424.7
Imports Goods and Services	502.0
Income Receipts	355.2
Income Payments	315.6
Unilateral Transfers (Net)	4.7
Total Current Account Flows	**1,602.**
Current Account Balance	**-42.1**

Source: U.S. Department of Commerce. Bureau of Economic Analysis. *U.S. International Transactions Accounts Data.* January 28, 2009. http://www.bea.doc.gov.

Table 3 indicates that the United States has consistently run surpluses in services trade with the EU. These surpluses helped, albeit modestly, to offset the U.S. merchandise trade deficits.

A substantial amount of funds flows between the United States and the EU as receipts of income derived from assets, including direct and portfolio investments and government securities. In 2007, $355.2 billion flowed to the United States from income earned on EU assets held by U.S. residents. In 2007, $315.6 billion flowed to the EU as income earned on assets held in the United States by EU residents. In addition, a net $4.7 billion flowed into the EU as unilateral transfers. Trade in goods and services, plus income receipts and payments, plus unilateral transfers, make up the U.S. **current account**, the most comprehensive measure of U.S. trade flows. In 2007, the United States incurred a **current account deficit** with the EU of $42.1 billion.[7]

In sum, the flows of merchandise or goods trade, services trade, and income between the United States and the EU manifest a very active, strong, and large economic relationship. In 2007 alone, a total of more than $1,602.2 billion flowed between the United States and the EU.[8]

U.S.-EU INVESTMENT FLOWS AND POSITIONS

Transactions on the current account represented only a part of the volume of international financial *flows* between the United States and EU in 2007. The remaining transactions are on the *capital account* which derive from payments by the U.S. government and residents to obtain assets in the EU and by EU residents to obtain assets in the United States.[9] These assets include government purchases of gold and foreign currencies for their official reserves and government purchases of other foreign assets. The capital account also includes payments by U.S. residents for portfolio investments (including bank deposits, government securities, corporate stocks, and bonds, and other private sector securities) and payments to obtain direct investments (including real estate, plants, factories, and commercial establishments). In 2007, the net flow of U.S. capital to EU members was $868.1 billion and the net flow of capital from EU countries into the United States was $1,019.0 billion.[10]

Foreign direct investments (FDI) represent long-term commitments on the part of the investor. In 2007, a net $175.5 billion *flowed* from U.S. residents to EU countries into direct investments, while a net $148.4 billion *flowed* from EU residents to direct investments in the United States.[11] By the end of 2007 the *position* of U.S. direct investment in EU countries stood at $1,376.9 billion, or 49.3% of all foreign direct investment by U.S. residents.[12] Of that total, $239.4 billion, or 17.4%, was in the manufacturing sector. Another 21.3% was in banking and other financial establishments, and insurance firms. The United Kingdom – accounting for 29.0% – is by the far the largest destination of U.S. FDI in the EU followed by the Netherlands at 19.2%, Germany at 7.8%, and France at 5.0%. At the end of 2007, EU residents had foreign direct investments in the United States valued at $1,301.8 billion. The United Kingdom was the largest source of those investments with 31.6% of the total in 2007.[13]

CONCLUSIONS AND POLICY IMPLICATIONS

Foreign trade and investment data depict a strong, interdependent, and significant U.S.-EU bilateral economic relationship. It is a relationship that is likely to grow in importance as advancements in technology and other forces of globalization, plus the future enlargement of the EU, force more trade and investment barriers to fall. The expanded relationship is widely seen as bringing economic benefits to both sides in the form of wider choices of goods and services and greater investment opportunities.

But increasing economic interdependence brings challenges as well as benefits. U.S.-EU trade ties have been plagued by disputes that at times have reached the highest levels of policymaking. While these disputes have covered a range of sectors and issues, the most contentious and public have been related to trade in agricultural and agricultural-related products. The United

States has taken the EU to task for its ban on hormone-enhanced beef imports and for its policy regarding banana imports.

Yet, the agriculture sector accounts for a very small portion of not only U.S.-EU bilateral trade but also for the total world trade of the two entities. In 2007, agriculture accounted for 4.0 % of total U.S. exports to the EU and for 5.5% of total imports from the EU. Similarly, in 2007 agriculture accounted for 8.3% of total U.S. world exports and for 6.1% of total EU world exports.[14] It is beyond the scope of this chapter to analyze this contrast between U.S. and EU trade policies and trade volume. But the contrast suggests that the attention received by these disputes at the official level, as well as from the press, reflects the domestic political salience of these issues to a much further extent than their overall commercial or economic significance.

Greater economic integration also challenges long-held notions of "sovereignty," as national or regional policies have extraterritorial impact. For example, the U.S. use of foreign policy trade sanctions against such "rogue states" as Cuba and Iran affected EU firms and investors and caused sharp U.S.-EU friction. Similarly, accepted understandings of "competition," "markets," and other economic concepts are tested as national borders dissolve with closer integration of economies.

U.S. and EU policymakers, therefore, continually face the task of how to manage the increasingly complex bilateral economic relationship in ways that maximize benefits and keep frictions to a minimum. For Members of Congress it means weighing the benefits and costs to constituents of greater economic integration and placing this calculation in the context of overall U.S. national interests.

End Notes

[1] The EU consists of Austria, Belgium, Bulgaria, Cyprus (Greek), Czech Republic, Denmark, Estonia, Finland, France, Germany, Greece, Hungary, Ireland, Italy, Latvia, Lithuania, Luxembourg, Malta, Netherlands, Poland, Portugal, Romania ,Slovakia, Slovenia, Spain, Sweden, and the United Kingdom.

[2] For more information on U.S.-EU disputes, see CRS Report RL3 0732, *Trade Conflict and the U.S.-European Union Economic Relationship*, by Raymond J. Ahearn.

[3] CIA. *World Factbook*. 2008. http://www.cia.org.

[4] But even the dominance of national security concerns did not prevent at least some major disputes to surface between the United States and the EU. For example, in June 1982, the United States imposed controls on exports to the Soviet Union of oil and gas equipment technology that was produced by U.S.-owned firms in foreign countries. The restrictions were in response to Soviet support of martial law in Poland and to hamper the construction of a natural gas pipeline that would deliver Soviet gas to Western Europe. The measures led

to an open confrontation with the European Community which argued that the United States could not apply U.S. controls outside the United States. The United States rescinded the controls in November 1982. Featherstone, Kevin and Roy H. Ginsburg. *The United States and the European Community in the 1990s: Partners in Transition*. St. Martin's Press. United Kingdom. 1993. p. 179- 180.

[5] Calculations for U.S. trade based on data from the U.S. Department of Commerce. Bureau of the Census. EU trade data from Eurostat. Both sets of data were compiled by Global Trade Information Systems, Inc. as part of World Trade Atlas.

[6] U.S. Department of Commerce. Bureau of Economic Analysis. *U.S. International Transactions Accounts Data*. October 16, 2007.

[7]. U.S. Department of Commerce. Bureau of Economic Analysis. *U.S. International Transactions Accounts Data*. October 16, 2007.

[8] Ibid.

[9] The Department of Commerce only reports net, rather than total, capital inflows and outflows. The capital account is also the mirror image of the current account in U.S. balance of payments accounts.

[10] U.S. Department of Commerce. Bureau of Economic Analysis. www.bea.gov.

[11] Ibid.

[12] The foreign investment *position* represents the value of total accumulated investments in place and is valued on an historical-cost basis, that is, the value at the time of purchase. Foreign investment flows represent the net value of investment transaction during a particular year.

[13] U.S. Department of Commerce. Bureau of Economic Analysis.

[14] Calculations made on data obtained from the U.S. Department of Agriculture's Foreign Agricultural Service and from Global Trade Information Systems, Inc., The World Trade Atlas.

In: European Union - U.S. Trade and Investment... ISBN: 978-1-60741-886-3
Editors: Linus R. Wilkens pp.83-120   © 2010 Nova Science Publishers, Inc.

Chapter 6

TRADE CONFLICT AND THE U.S.-EUROPEAN UNION ECONOMIC RELATIONSHIP

Raymond J. Ahearn

SUMMARY

The United States and the European Union (EU) share a huge, dynamic, and mutually beneficial economic partnership. Not only is the U.S.-EU trade and investment relationship the largest in the world, but it is also arguably the most important. Agreement between the two partners in the past has been critical to making the world trading system more open and efficient.

Given the high level of U.S.-EU commercial interactions, trade tensions and disputes are not unexpected. In the past, U.S.-EU trade relations have witnessed periodic episodes of rising trade tensions and conflicts, only to be followed by successful efforts at dispute settlement. This ebb and flow of trade tensions occurred again in 2006 with high-profile disputes involving the Doha Round of multilateral trade negotiations and production subsidies for the commercial aircraft sector.

Major U.S.-EU trade disputes have varied causes. Some disputes stem from demands from producer interests for support or protection. Trade conflicts involving agriculture, aerospace, steel, and 'contingency protection' fit prominently into this grouping. These conflicts tend to be prompted by traditional trade barriers such as subsidies, tariffs, or industrial policy instruments, where the economic dimensions of the conflict predominate. Other conflicts arise when the U.S. or the EU initiate actions or measures to protect or promote their political and economic interests, often in the absence of significant private sector pressures. The underlying cause of these disputes over such issues as sanctions, unilateral trade actions, and preferential trade agreements are different foreign policy goals and priorities of Brussels and Washington. Still other conflicts stem from an array of domestic regulatory policies that reflect differing social and environmental values and objectives. Conflicts over hormone-treated beef, bio-engineered food products, protection of the audio-visual sector, and aircraft hushkits, for example, are rooted in different U.S.-EU regulatory approaches, as well as social preferences.

These three categories of trade conflicts — traditional, foreign policy, and regulatory — possess varied potential for future trade conflict. This is due mostly to the fact that bilateral and multilateral agreements governing the settlement of disputes affect each category of disputes differently. By providing a fairly detailed map of permissible actions and obligations, trade agreements can dampen the inclination of governments to supply protection and private sector parties to demand protection.

In sum, U.S.-EU bilateral trade conflicts do not appear to be as ominous and threatening as the media often portray, but they are not ephemeral distractions either. Rather they appear to have real, albeit limited, economic and political consequences for the bilateral relationship. From an economic perspective, the disputes may also be weakening efforts of the two partners to provide strong leadership to the global trading system.

INTRODUCTION

The bilateral economic relationship between the United States and European Union (EU) is shaped by two outstanding trends. On the one hand, the two transatlantic economies share a high degree of commercial interaction, most notably a huge trade and investment relationship and a growing number of corporate mergers. Cooperation between the two partners has been critical to the promotion of world trade. On the other hand, the bilateral economic relationship is subject to limited, but increasingly contentious, trade conflicts that potentially could have adverse political and economic repercussions.[1]

---

[1] For the purposes of this chapter, the term "conflict" is used broadly to include U.S.-EU disagreements on issues that may not have been raised in formal World Trade Organization (WTO)

These include a weakening of shared interests and bonds as well as an undermining of the credibility of the World Trade Organization.

The dimensions of the mutually beneficial side of the economic relationship are well known. The United States and EU are parties to the largest two-way trade and investment relationship in the world. Annual two-way flows of goods, services, and foreign direct investment exceeded $1.3 trillion in 2005. This sum means that over $3 billion is spent every day on transatlantic purchases of goods, services, and direct investments.[2]

The European Union as a unit is the second largest (next to Canada) trading partner of the United States in merchandise or goods. In 2005 the EU accounted for 20.6% (or $186 billion) of U.S. exports and 18.5% (or $309 billion) of U.S. imports. The EU is also the largest U.S. trading partner in services. In 2005, the EU purchased slightly over 34% of total U.S. services exports (or $130 billion). But the United States since 1993 has been importing more goods from the EU than it has been exporting. In 2005, the resulting U.S. trade deficit with the EU totaled $122 billion or 16% of the U.S. merchandise trade deficit with the world. This trade deficit is partially offset by U.S. surpluses in services trade which have averaged around $10 billion dollars over the 2002-2005 period.

Based on a population of some 457 million citizens and a gross domestic product of about $13.4 trillion (compared to a U.S. population of 298 million and a GDP of $12.5 trillion in 2005), the twenty-five members of the EU combine to form the single largest (in terms of GDP) market in the world.[3] Given the reforms entailed in the introduction of the European single market in the early 1990s, along with the introduction of a single currency, the *euro*, for twelve members, the EU market is also increasingly open and standardized.

---

proceedings. The term "dispute" is used more narrowly for issues that have been subject to WTO consultations, including those requests which have led to panel and appellate review proceedings. Unless referring to a particular dispute, the two terms, however, are often used interchangeably.

[2] Data sources for this section, unless otherwise noted, are drawn from the following sources: Cooper, William H., *EU-U.S. Economic Ties: Framework, Scope, and Magnitude*, CRS Report RL30608; the European Union's profile of facts and figures on the EU-U.S. economic relationship found on-line at [http://www.eurunion.org/profile/facts]; and various editions of the Survey of Current Business, Department of Commerce.

[3] The addition of Bulgaria and Romania in January 2007 makes the EU a 27 country grouping with a population of nearly 500 million.

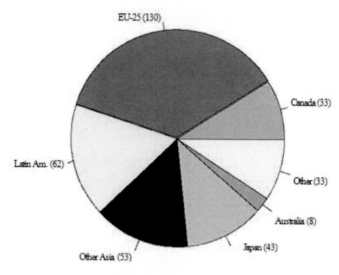

(Billions of U.S. Dollars)

Figure 1. U.S. Exports of Services by Region/Country, 2005

Source: U.S. Department of Commerce.

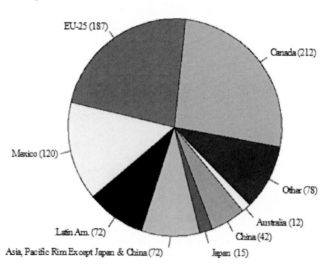

(Billions of U.S. Dollars)

Figure 2. U.S. Exports of Goods by Region/Country, 2005

Source: U.S. Department of Commerce.

The fact that each side has a major ownership stake in the other's market may be the most remarkable aspect of the commercial relationship. At the end of 2004, the total stock of two-way direct investment reached $1.9 trillion (composed of $942 billion in EU investment in the United States and $965 billion in U.S. investment in the EU), making U.S. and European companies the largest investors in each other's market. Roughly 60% of corporate America's foreign investments are located in Europe, while almost 75% of Europe's foreign investments are based in the United States. This massive amount of ownership of companies in each other's markets translates into billions of dollars of sales, production, and expenditures on research and development. In addition, an estimated 6-7 million Americans are employed by European affiliates operating in the United States and almost an equal number of EU citizens work for American companies in Europe.[4]

Foreign direct investment also serves to spur international trade flows. This is due to the fact that trade taking place within the same company (imports by U.S. affiliates from their EU parent firms and exports by U.S. companies to their EU affiliates) accounts for around one-third of U.S. total trade with the EU. The trade and employment linkages associated with foreign direct investment engender strong and politically active interest groups that lobby on both sides of the Atlantic in favor of maintaining friendly bilateral ties, reducing regulations, and in opposing protectionist proposals.

The United States and the European Union, acting in concert, are the superpowers of the world trading system. As shown in **Tables 1 and 2**, together they accounted for 35% of world merchandise trade in 2004 and 60% of the world's production of goods and services in 2003. Cooperation and joint leadership between the two partners have historically been the key to all efforts to liberalize world trade on a multilateral basis, including the creation of the General Agreement on Tariffs and Trade (GATT) in 1948 and the World Trade Organization (WTO) in 1995.

---

[4] Hamilton, Daniel S. and Joseph P. Quinlan, *Partners in Prosperity: The Changing Geography of the Transatlantic Economy,* The Johns Hopkins University, 2004.

Table 1. World Merchandise Trade, 2004
(Excluding intra-EU trade)
(Billions of U.S. Dollars)

	Imports and Exports	% of Total
United States	2,343	17.2
EU-25	2,483	18.2
U.S. and EU-25	4,826	35.4
World	13,627	100

Source: WTO.

Table 2. World Gross Domestic Product, 2003
(Billions of Dollars)

Region/Country	GDP	% of World Total
United States	10,949	30.0
EU-25	10,959	30.0
EU-25 plus United States	21,908	60.0
Japan	4,301	11.7
Latin America & Caribbean	1,740	4.7
East Asia and Pacific	2,033	6.6
China + Hong Kong	1,574	5.6
Canada	856	2.3
Middle East and N. Africa	745	2.0
South Asia	765	2.0
Sub -Saharan Africa	439	1.2
World	36,461	100

Source: World Bank, World Development Indicators - 2005.

Trade tensions, disputes, and rivalry coexist alongside and, in part, result from these cooperative and generally positive currents. Bilateral trade disputes have been an important part of the relationship during the Cold War as well as after. They are nothing new nor unexpected given the huge volume of commercial interactions. Historically, with the possible exception of agriculture, the disputes have been managed without excessive political rancor, perhaps due to the balanced nature of the trade and investment relationship. Policymakers and many academics often emphasize that the U.S. and EU always have more in common than in dispute, and like to point out that trade disputes usually affect a tiny fraction (often estimated at 1-2 percent) of the trade in goods and services.

All In the Family?

The notion that trade disputes with the European Union generally have engendered less political rancor and bitterness than U.S. trade disputes with a number of developing countries and Japan is a popular one. Whether the proposition is valid or not, the most common explanation put forth relates to the view that transatlantic trade relations are underpinned by comparable levels of socioeconomic development and by more balanced economic interactions.

EU member states, unlike many developing countries, have wage rates and labor and environmental standards that equal or exceed U.S. standards. From one perspective, this fact shields Europe from charges of "cutthroat" competition and "unfair" trade that are often directed at low-wage developing countries possessing relatively low labor and environmental standards.

Several indicators support the argument that trade between the United States and EU takes place on a "level playing field." As measured by the value of imports and exports of goods and services as a percentage of GDP, for example, a case can be made that both economies are similarly open to trade. In 2005, the trade openness ratios of both trading partners ranged between 25 and 30 percent.

The composition of trade and pattern of trade deficits are also used to illustrate that U.S.-EU trade ties are balanced and non-adversarial. Unlike U.S. trade with China, U.S.- EU trade is characterized by a high level of intra-industry trade, where both sides import and export similar products such as cars, computers, aircraft, and integrated circuits. Nor have U.S. merchandise trade deficits with the EU given rise to the same kind of concern that U.S. trade deficits with China have sparked. Macroeconomic factors, such as differential economic growth rates and the exchange rates, are generally thought to explain most of the fluctuation in the U.S.-EU bilateral deficit, rather than trade barriers or other structural attributes.

In the middle of this decade, however, Washington and Brussels are still at loggerheads over a number of issues, ranging from bio-engineered food products and aircraft to the treatment of agriculture in the Doha Round of multilateral trade negotiations. The conflicts have not been easy to resolve, and some of the efforts at dispute resolution have led to escalation and tit-for-tat retaliation. Instead of compromising in an effort to find solutions, policymakers on both sides sometimes appear more interested in getting even.

Congress has been in the middle of many of the trade disputes. By both crafting and passing legislation, Congress has supported the efforts of U.S. agricultural and industrial interests to gain better access to EU markets. Congress has pressured the executive branch to take a harder line against the EU in resolving a number of disputes, but has also cooperated with the Administration in crafting compromise solutions.

Combined with a growing value of trade now being disputed, the political and economic effects of trade discord between Brussels and Washington are important questions. Why are many disputes so difficult to resolve? What can be done to improve dispute resolution efforts? Are the disputes undermining business confidence or efforts at economic policy coordination? Are the disputes weakening the credibility of the WTO dispute settlement system? Do the political disputes reflect differences between the two partners in terms of basic values and orientations? If so, could the disputes force a fundamental re-evaluation of the importance of the bilateral relationship? In short, what is the significance of trade conflict to the bilateral relationship?

This chapter considers these overriding questions in three parts. The first part categorizes and evaluates the trade conflicts according to their underlying causes and characteristics. In light of the causes and dimensions of the disputes, the second section examines the potential for conflict management. A final section assesses the role that trade disputes may be playing in the U.S.-EU economic relationship.

SOURCES OF TRADE CONFLICT

Changes in government regulations, laws, or practices that protect or promote domestic commercial interests at the expense of foreign interests are at the heart of most trade conflicts. While governments are the sole providers or suppliers of trade protection, there are a range of parties or interest groups that demand or request measures that result in protection for domestic parties. These include producers and workers, as well as consumer and environmental interest groups. Governments may also be the primary demanders or initiators of actions that have trade protectionist effects.

U.S.-EU trade conflicts vary according to the nature of the demand for protection. Many of the major U.S.-EU trade conflicts are classified and discussed below according to the nature of the demand for protective action. While many of the conflicts are spurred by multiple demanders and causes, an attempt is made to classify disputes according to categories that seemingly account for the overriding cause or demand for government action.

As most trade conflicts embody a mixture of economic, political, and social dimensions, there is ample room for disagreement over the dominant cause of any particular dispute. By and large, this chapter classifies most of the conflicts according to American perspectives. U.S.-European disagreements over the cause and nature of the controversy, of course, provides the basis for many of the conflicts. Whether the conflict is propelled by protectionist or other domestic aims remains a key question in some disputes as well.

TRADITIONAL TRADE CONFLICT: PRODUCER PROTECTION

Some conflicts stem primarily from demands from producer or vested interests for protection or state aids. These kinds of disagreements arise when both transatlantic trade partners, in support of vested interests and key industries, craft policies that try to open markets for exports but keep markets protected from imports as much as possible. Trade conflicts involving agriculture, aerospace, steel, and 'contingency protection' fit prominently in this grouping. These are examples of traditional trade conflicts, prompted by trade barriers such as tariffs, subsidies or industrial policy instruments, where the economic dimensions of the conflict predominate.

Agriculture. Agricultural trade disputes historically have been major sticking points in transatlantic relations. Accounting for a declining percentage of output and employment in both the EU and United States, the agricultural sector has produced a disproportionate amount of the trade tension between the two sides. In the past, the majority of what can be called traditional conflicts stemmed primarily from government efforts to shield or protect farmers from the full effects of market forces (non-traditional agricultural disputes involving food safety and the application of biotechnology to food production are discussed below under **Regulatory Protection**).

From the U.S. perspective, the restrictive trade regime set up by the Common Agricultural Policy (CAP) has been the real villain. It has been a longstanding U.S. contention that the CAP is the largest single distortion of global agricultural trade. American farmers and policymakers have complained over the years that U.S. sales and profits are adversely affected by (1) EU restrictions on market access that have protected the European market for European farmers; (2) by EU export subsidies that have deflated U.S. sales to third markets; and (3) by EU domestic income support programs that have kept non-competitive European farmers in business.[5]

Agricultural conflict, particularly over the decline in U.S. exports to the EU and growing EU competition for sales in third markets, was intense in the 1 980s. During this period, the majority of U.S. Section 301 cases were directed at the CAP and fierce subsidy wars were waged over third country markets. Acrimonious agricultural subsidy disputes over canned fruit, oilseeds, wine, wheat flour, pasta, sugar, and poultry between the two sides tested the GATT dispute settlement system to its limits in the 1980s.[6]

What Is The CAP?

The Common Agricultural Policy of the EU is a domestically-oriented farm policy whose primary objective is supporting farm income. Since its inception in 1962, the CAP has been guided by three principles: (1) a free flow of agricultural commodities within the EU; (2) community preferences whereby EU products have priority in the internal market over imports; and (3) common financing of agricultural programs.

Historically, the high support prices of the CAP have provided strong incentives for investing in EU agriculture. Since 1970, the EU has shifted from being a net importer to one of the world's largest net exporters of wheat, sugar, beef, pork, poultry, and dairy products.

One effect of the CAP has been to raise overall food prices for consumers in the EU. Most U.S. farm programs, in contrast, support farm income without raising food prices to the consumer.

Spending on the CAP accounts for over 50 percent of the EU budget. High budget outlays in the past have caused several budget "crises," leading to policy reforms aimed at curbing agricultural expenditures. EU enlargement to include

---

[5] For a comparison of agricultural programs, see Becker, Geoffrey S. Agricultural Support Mechanisms in the European Union: A Comparison with the United States. CRS Report RL30753.

[6] Section 301 of the Trade Act of 1974, as amended, requires the United States Trade Representative to take all appropriate action, including retaliation, to obtain the removal of any act, policy, or practice of a foreign government that violates an international agreement or is unjustifiable, unreasonable or discriminatory, and burdens and restricts U.S. commerce. In practice, it has been employed mostly on behalf of American exporters fighting foreign import barriers or subsidized competition in third-country markets.

a number of East European countries that have large agricultural sectors is providing additional pressures for reforming the CAP.

Tensions, however, have moderated markedly since the completion of the Uruguay Round in the mid-1990s. The 1994 Uruguay Round Agreement on Agriculture defined more clearly what both partners can do in their agricultural and trade policies, as well as defined more clearly the quantities of agricultural products that countries can export with subsidies and strengthened the procedure for settling disputes involving those rules. The agreement also contained a nine-year "peace clause" whereby WTO members agreed not to challenge other countries' subsidies with domestic cases or WTO challenges.[7]

For the most part, the U.S. and EU have honored their Uruguay Round agricultural commitments, including 'due restraint.' Scope for future conflict has been constrained, or perhaps redirected into areas not so clearly covered by the Agreement of Agriculture. These included a number of non-traditional disputes over beef hormones, bio-engineered food products, and geographical indicators — none of which involved domestic subsidies.[8]

Negotiations on agriculture in the Doha Round have continued to divide the two economic superpowers. The United States has proposed substantial reductions in domestic subsidies, expanded market access through both tariff reduction and expansion of market access quotas, and the elimination of export subsidies. The EU, for its part, has called on the United States to increase its offer to reduce trade- distorting domestic support but has not been willing to improve its offer to expand market access. Unless these positions can be bridged, the negotiations may remain deadlocked.

Aerospace.[9] Claims and counter-claims concerning government support for the aviation industry have been a major source of friction in U.S.-EU relations over the past several decades. The fights have focused primarily on EU member state support for Airbus Industrie, a consortium of four European companies that collectively produce Airbus aircraft. According to the Office of the U.S. Trade Representative (USTR), Airbus member governments (France, U.K.,

---

[7] Tangermann, Stefan. "The Common and Uncommon Agricultural Policies," In *Transatlantic Relations in A Global Economy,* Mayer, Otto and Scharrer, Hans-Eckart, eds, Nomos Verlagsgesellschaft, 1999, p. 143.

[8] T. Josling and S. Tangermann, "Production and Export Subsidies in Agriculture: Lessons from GATT and WTO Disputes Involving the US and the EC," In Ernst-Ulrich Petersmann and Mark A. Pollack, *Transatlantic Economic Disputes: The EU, the US, and the WTO,* Oxford University Press, 2003. p 224.

[9] This section was written by John W. Fischer, Specialist in Transportation, Resources, Science, and Industry Division.

Germany and Spain) have provided massive subsidies since 1967 to their member companies to aid in the development, production, and marketing of the Airbus family of large civil aircraft. The U.S. has also accused the EU of providing other forms of support to gain an unfair advantage in this key sector, including equity infusions, debt forgiveness, debt rollovers, marketing assistance, and favored access to EU airports and airspace.[10]

For its part, the EU has long resisted U.S. charges and argued that for strategic and economic purposes it could not cede the entire passenger market to the Americans, particularly in the wake of the 1997 Boeing-McDonnell Douglas merger and the pressing need to maintain sufficient global competition. The Europeans have also counter-charged that their actions are justified because U.S. aircraft producers have benefitted from huge indirect governmental subsidies in the form of military and space contracts and government sponsored aerospace research and development.[11]

The most recent round of this longstanding trade dispute stems from a May 30, 2005 WTO filing by the United States alleging that European Community (EC) Member States provided Airbus with illegal subsidies giving the firm an unfair advantage in the world market for large commercial jet aircraft. The following day the EC submitted its own request to the WTO claiming that Boeing had received illegal subsidies from the U.S. government. Two panels were established on October 17, 2005 (one handling the U.S. charges against Airbus and the other handling the EU's counterclaims against Boeing), and both panels have begun hearing the cases. Final panel rulings are not expected to be handed down until October 31, 2007, at the earliest.

Much of the ongoing debate about the Airbus/Boeing relationship stems from Airbus's December 2000 launch of a program to construct the world's largest commercial passenger aircraft, the Airbus A380. The A380 is being offered in several passenger versions seating between 500 and 800 passengers, and as a freighter. At the end of 2005, Airbus was listing 159 firm orders for the aircraft from 16 different airlines.[12] The project is believed to have cost about $13 billion, which includes some significant cost overruns identified by Airbus in 2005. Airbus expects that its member firms will provide 60% of this sum, with the remaining 40% coming from subcontractors. State-aid from European governments is also a source of funding for Airbus member firms.

---

[10] USTR National Trade Estimates Report: 2000, pp. 102-104.

[11] Burger, Bettina. "Transatlantic Economic Relations: Common Interests and Conflicts in High Technology and Industrial Policies," In *Transatlantic Relations in A Global Economy*, p. 110.

[12] [http://www.speednews.com/lists/05O&D.pdf]

State-aid is limited to one-third of the project's total cost by the 1992 Agreement on Government Support for Civil Aircraft between the United States and the European Union (EU) (now repudiated by the United States, but not by the EC).

Shortly after the A380 project was announced, Boeing dropped its support of a competing new large aircraft. Boeing believes that the market for A380-size aircraft is limited. It has, therefore, settled on the concept of producing a new technology 250-seat aircraft, the 787, which is viewed as a replacement for 767-size aircraft.[13] The 787 is designed to provide point-to-point service on a wide array of possible international and domestic U.S. routes. The aircraft design incorporates features such as increased use of composite materials in structural elements and new engines, with the goal of producing an aircraft that is significantly more fuel efficient than existing aircraft types. Boeing formally launched the program in 2004 and obtained 56 firm orders during the remainder of 2004. By the end of 2005 the order book for the 787 had expanded dramatically to 291 aircraft.

To construct this aircraft Boeing is proposing to greatly expand its use of nonU.S. subcontractors and non-traditional funding. For example, a Japanese group will provide approximately 35% of the funding for the project ($1.6 billion). In return this group will produce a large portion of the aircraft's structure and the wings (this will be the first time that a Boeing commercial product will use a non-U.S. built wing). Alenia of Italy is expected to provide $600 million and produce the rear fuselage of the aircraft. In each of these instances, the subcontractor is expected to receive some form of financial assistance from their respective governments. Other subcontractors are also expected to take large financial stakes in the new aircraft. The project is also expected to benefit from state and local tax and other incentives. Most notable among these is $3.2 billion of such incentives from the state of Washington. Many of these non-traditional funding arrangements are specifically cited by the EC in its WTO complaint as being illegal subsidies.

Whether the WTO litigation provides an incentive for the United States and the EU to resolve the dispute bilaterally remains to be seen. To date the two sides have wrangled over a host of procedural issues, but have not been negotiating on a possible settlement to the dispute. Some analysts believe that as long as the dispute is not resolved, Boeing can use Airbus subsidies as an

---

[13] Boeing has rethought its position on the large aircraft market. On November 14, 2005 Boeing launched the 747-8, a new stretched derivative of the venerable 747. It has received 18 orders for the aircraft in freighter configuration, but is expected to produce a passenger version of the aircraft as well.

argument for securing a lucrative U.S. Air Force contract for refueling tankers. Other analysts speculate that Airbus' weakened business condition brought on by the delivery delays of its jumbo A380 plane may also be a reason why Boeing may not be pressing the U.S. government to settle the case.

Steel. Conflict over trade in steel products has occurred sporadically over the past two decades. Although the EU industry has undergone significant consolidation and privatization in the 1990s, the U.S. government in the past has alleged that many EU companies still benefit from earlier state subsidies and/or engage in dumping steel products (selling at "less than fair value") in foreign markets. U.S. steel companies also have aggressively used U.S. trade laws to fight against EU steel imports by filing antidumping and countervailing duty petitions that include imports from EU countries. In return, the EU has countered with numerous challenges in the WTO against the alleged U.S. misuse of its countervailing duty and antidumping laws.

In addition to "unfair" trade disputes, President Bush in June 2001 requested the U.S. International Trade Commission (ITC) undertake a new Section 201 trade investigation on the steel industry.[14] The petition had broad support from Congress, the steel industry, and labor unions. The ITC subsequently ruled that much of the industry was being injured by increased imports and recommended relief measures to President Bush. On March 5, 2003, the President decided to impose three-year safeguard tariffs with top rates of 30%. He imposed the restrictions for three years on all major steel exporting countries except U.S. free trade partners such as Canada and Mexico.

The U.S. decision raised cries of indignation and protectionism from European leaders, and prompted a quick response. On March 27, 2002, citing a threat of diversion of steel from the U.S. market to Europe, the EU announced provisional tariffs of 15% to 26% on 15 different steel products. The EU and a number of other countries adversely affected by the U.S. tariffs also formally challenged the U.S. action as being inconsistent with WTO rules.

In early 2003 a WTO panel determined that the U.S. action had a number of shortcomings. The panel found that the United States had failed to adequately demonstrate that rising imports were injuring the U.S. industry. In September 2003, the ITC issued its mid-term report of the safeguards, and determined that termination of the measures was warranted. This determination, in turn,

---

[14] Section 201 relief, often referred to as "safeguard," provides for temporary restrictions on imports that have surged in such quantities as to cause or threaten to cause serious injury to a domestic industry. The procedure is compatible with the rules of the WTO. A Section 201 case does not in itself need to demonstrate dumping, subsidization, or other unfair practices by U.S. trading partners.

provided President Bush with leeway to avoid further international conflict by terminating the steel safeguard measures on December 5, 2003.

Contingency Protection. A variety of legal procedures, sanctioned by the WTO, provides domestic producers temporary protection against both "fair" and "unfair" trade practices. These include safeguard or import relief procedures for fair trade and anti-dumping and countervailing procedures for unfair trade practices. While these procedures are sanctioned by the WTO, and often referred to as contingency protection, either side's implementation of these procedures is often controversial.

A case in point has been the Continued Dumping and Subsidy Offset Act (CDSOA), or Byrd Amendment. Enacted by the U.S. Congress in October 2000, this provision required that the proceeds from antidumping and countervailing duty cases be paid to the U.S. companies responsible for bringing the cases, instead of to the U.S. Treasury. Soon after enactment, the EU and eight other parties challenged the statute in the WTO on the grounds that the provision constituted a "non-permissible specific action against dumping or a subsidy" contrary to various WTO agreements. Basically, the plaintiffs argued that the action benefitted U.S. companies doubly: first, by the imposition of the antidumping or countervailing duties and, second, by receiving the duties at the expense of their competitors.

The WTO in January 2003 concluded that the Byrd Amendment was an impermissible action against dumping or subsidization and gave the United States until December 23, 2003, to comply with the WTO ruling. When the United States did not comply with the ruling, the complaining members requested authorization to impose retaliatory measures. A WTO arbitrator determined in August 2004 that each of the eight complainants could impose countermeasures on an annual basis in an amount equal to 72% of the CDSOA disbursements for the most recent year in which U.S. data are available.

Canada and the EU began retaliating on May 2, 2005, by placing a 15% additional duty on selected U.S. exports. Mexico imposed higher tariffs on U.S. milk products, wine, and chewing gum, and Japan placed an additional tariff of 15% on 15 steel and industrial products.

Despite strong congressional support for the Byrd Amendment in both chambers, a provision repealing the CDSOA was included in the conference report to S. 1932, the Deficit Reduction Act of 2005, and approved in February 2006. The repeal however, allowed CDSOA payments on all goods that enter the United States to continue through October 1, 2007. As a result, the EU, Canada, and Mexico indicated their intention to keep the sanctions on U.S. imports in place as long as the disbursements continue. The EU, in particular, elected to increase the amount of retaliation by nearly $9 million (from $27.8 million to

$36.9 million) and expand the list of products that will face punitive duties. U.S. trade officials and some Members of Congress have expressed disappointment and frustration that retaliation was not lifted in the wake of the Byrd repeal.[15]

FOREIGN POLICY CONFLICT: CLASHING STATE INTERESTS

This category comprises conflicts where the United States or the European Union has initiated actions or measures to protect or promote their political and economic interests, often in the absence of significant private sector pressures. The underlying causes of these disputes are quite different foreign policy goals and priorities, if not interests. Most of these conflicts have important economic interests at stake, but seldom are the economic stakes viewed as the overriding cause or explanation of the action that ostensibly precipitated the disagreement.

From the EU perspective, extraterritorial provisions of U.S. sanctions legislation and unilateralism in U.S. trade legislation are concerns that fit into this category. From a U.S. perspective, the EU's preferential dealings with third countries, the Foreign Sales Corporation (FSC) export tax-rebate dispute, and challenges to varied U.S. trade laws could be said to be driven primarily by EU foreign policy priorities.

EU Concerns. U.S. legislation which requires the imposition of trade sanctions for foreign policy or non-trade reasons has been a major concern of the EU. While the EU often shares many of the foreign policy goals of the United States that are addressed in such legislation, it has opposed the extraterritorial provisions of certain pieces of U.S. legislation that seek to unilaterally regulate or control trade and investment activities conducted by companies outside the United States. Although these issues have been relatively quiet in recent years, a number of the provisions remain U.S. law, including the Cuban Liberty and Democratic Solidarity Act of 1996 (so-called Helms-Burton Act) and the Iran Libya Sanctions Act (ILSA), which threaten the extraterritorial imposition of U.S. sanctions against European firms doing business in Cuba, Iran, and

---

[15] *Inside U.S. Trade,* "EU Expands Byrd Retaliation Duties; Canada Undecided On Options," April 28, 2006.

Libya.[16] Other EU concerns about different instances of U.S. extra-territoriality relate to various environmentally driven embargoes, export control legislation, and sub-federal (states) procurement provisions or boycott activities.[17]

The Helms-Burton Act, passed in 1996 after the Cuban military shot down two small U.S. based civilian planes, led to a firestorm of protest in Europe. Perhaps not since the U.S. imposed sanctions against companies doing business on a Russian pipeline in the early 1980s had the European outcry been so vociferous. The bill, which was designed to further isolate Cuba economically, imposed a secondary boycott against foreign nationals and companies that "traffic "in Cuban-expropriated properties formerly owned by U.S. nationals.[18]

Maintaining that Helms-Burton is extraterritorial and a violation of WTO rules, the EU passed countervailing legislation against its enforcement and initiated a WTO panel investigation. The U.S. responded by claiming the WTO lacked competence to investigate the matter because Helms-Burton is a "national security" issue and therefore should qualify for a waiver under section 21 of the GATT. After a year of high-level political negotiations, an understanding was reached in April 1997 that charted a longer-term solution through negotiation of international disciplines and principles for greater protection of foreign investment, combined with the proposed amendment of the Helms-Burton Act. At the May 1998 EU-U.S. Summit, the United States agreed to either implement or seek measures that would protect EU companies from any penalties called for in Helms-Burton and Iran-Libya Sanction Act.[19] Formal implementation of the Understanding, however, still awaits legislative action by Congress.[20]

Closely related to EU concerns about extraterritoriality are complaints about U.S. trade laws and procedures that allow for the "unilateral" imposition of trade sanctions against offending countries or companies. Most EU complaints relate to the "Section 301" family of trade provisions which

---

[16] The application of ILSA with respect to Libya was terminated by President Bush in April 2004.

[17] The EU has been particularly critical of efforts by U.S. states and cities to limit government procurement opportunities as a result of the companies' business links with particular foreign countries. A law adopted by Massachusetts focused on corporate involvement with Burma had been a considerable concern until it was overturned by the Supreme Court on June 19, 2000.

[18] This provision has been waived by Presidents Clinton and Bush annually since its enactment.

[19] "EU, Spain Warn U.S. of Action Over Helms-Burton Cuba Measure," *International Trade Reporter,* August 18, 1999, p. 1364.

[20] EU Annual Report on U.S. Trade Barriers, 2005, p.1.

authorize the executive branch to impose trade sanctions in an effort to enforce U.S. rights under international trade agreements and to combat foreign unfair trade practices. In addition to general trade barriers which the U.S. government deems discriminate against or burden U.S. commerce, other more specialized provisions dealing with government procurement barriers (often legislated by states) and intellectual property rights violations are also subject to EU charges as examples of U.S. unilateralism.

Additionally upsetting to some American interests, the EU during the 1997- 2000 period filed a number of mostly technical challenges in the WTO to a variety of U.S. trade statutes, including Section 301, a law (section 337) dealing with the protection of intellectual property rights, and the U.S. antidumping laws. Some Americans view these WTO challenges as part of a systematic and concerted EU strategy to weaken or gut U.S. trade laws, perhaps in an effort to gain negotiating leverage that could be used in future efforts to arrive a transatlantic consensus on the agenda for a new round of multilateral trade negotiations.[21]

U.S. Complaints. The United States in the past has expressed concerns about the discriminatory impact of preferential agreements the EU has negotiated with third countries. These include preferential trade agreements with prospective EU members in Eastern and Central Europe and with developing countries in Africa and the Caribbean. As a result of these agreements, only eight countries including the United States, Japan and Canada, now receive MFN treatment for their exports to EU.

Some U.S. observers have also worried that enlargement and institutional deepening have become EU policy goals that are limiting its commitment to global trade liberalization. Under this view, the EU's "internal" preoccupation translates into less interest in negotiating any new MFN or WTO obligations because such obligations could intensify adjustment pressures EU firms are experiencing as a result of the drive toward a single market and the heightened import competition resulting from preferential tariff agreements negotiated with various regional trading partners. At the same time, the United States has also supported both enlargement and deepening in the political interest of "European stability," thus raising a question concerning the compatibility of U.S. political and trade goals.

---

[21] Statement of Senator Max Baucus, "Improving U.S. Trade Law," Conference on America's Trade Agenda After the Battle in Seattle, July 20, 2000.

For its part, the EU has expressed fears that free trade agreements being pursued by the United States could lead to discrimination against its exports. Specifically, the EU is concerned that U.S. efforts to negotiate free trade agreements with Asia through the Asian Pacific Economic Cooperation (APEC) process and with Latin America through the Free Trade Area of the Americas (FTAA) could lead to discrimination against EU exports. This, in turn, has been a spur for the EU to negotiate its own free trade accords with Mexico, and the Mercosur countries of Latin America.

A different U.S. concern relates to the Foreign Sales Corporation (FSC) provisions of the U.S. tax code. This provision allowed U.S. firms to exempt between 15% and 30% of export income from taxation by sheltering some income in offshore foreign sales corporations. General Electric, Boeing, Motorola, Caterpillar, Allied Signal, Cisco, Monsanto, and Archer Daniels Midland were among the top beneficiaries of this arrangement.[22]

The FSC was enacted in 1984 to replace the Domestic International Sales Corporation (DISC) — a different tax benefit for exporting that the EU had successfully challenged in the GATT. Both provisions were designed to stimulate the U.S. economy through increased exports. While the European officials may not have been fully satisfied that the FSC was fully GATT legal, they nevertheless waited thirteen years (until November 1997) to take the first steps to challenge the scheme under the WTO dispute settlement system.

The EU argued that it challenged the FSC because it violated WTO subsidy obligations, distorted international competition, and provided U.S. exporters unfair advantages. Yet, with the possible exception of Airbus, the Brussels challenge appeared to have very limited backing from European business.[23] A number of European subsidiaries operating in the United States, in fact, benefitted from the FSC.

A more common explanation is that the EU challenge had more to do with an attempt to gain negotiating leverage over the United States, as well as with getting even for U.S. pressures over beef and bananas, than to redress a perceived commercial disadvantage. A *Financial Times* editorial viewed the challenge as "titfor-tat retaliation for U.S. bullying in trade disputes over

---

[22] CRS Report RS20746, Export Tax Benefits and the WTO: The Extraterritorial Income Exclusion and Foreign Sales Corporations, by David L. Brumbaugh.

[23] One source cites Airbus Industrie's concerns in the early 1990s over the FSC benefits Boeing was receiving. See Airline Business, "Flying FSCs Anger Airbus," May 1993, p. 21.

bananas and beef. Having won its point, the EU now seems determined — in the name of upholding trade rules — to make the U.S. squirm."[24]

The EU challenge was successful, with the requirement that the United States bring the FSC provisions in conformity with the WTO by October 2000. Following the ruling, Congress passed the replacement extraterritorial income (ETI) tax provision, but this law was also found inconsistent with WTO obligations in 2002. Subsequently, the WTO authorized the EU to retaliate in the absence of U.S. compliance, and the EU began imposing escalating retaliatory duties (starting at 5%) on $4 billion of U.S. exports on March 1, 2004. After reaching 14% in December 2004, these sanctions were lifted in January 2005 subsequent to congressional repeal of the FSC/ETI provisions in the American Jobs Creation Act (P.L. 108-357) of October 2004. But a WTO ruling of February 13, 2006, determined that the act perpetuated the illegal subsidies with a two-year phase-out of the tax breaks and a grandfather clause covering exporters that had sales contracts dated before September 17, 2003.

In announcing the EU's decision to reimpose sanctions, Peter Mandelson, the EU's top trade official, said that "the EU will not accept a system of tax benefits which give U.S. exporters, including Boeing, unfair advantage against their European competitors." But the reimposition of the tariffs was avoided when President Bush on May 17, 2006, signed a tax bill that among other things repealed the grandfathered FSC/ETI benefits.

REGULATORY POLICY CONFLICT: SOCIAL AND ENVIRONMENTAL PROTECTION

This category of conflict deals with an array of domestic policies, including regulations and standards, that produce conflict by altering the terms of competition in the name of promoting social, cultural, or environmental objectives. Often domestic producers benefit, either intentionally or inadvertently, at the expense of foreign producers. Many of these clashes have occurred as a result of efforts by both partners to strengthen food safety and environmental standards; others have occurred as a result of the EU's need to harmonize standards in support of its drive towards a single market. Still others have occurred as a result of a drive to maintain or promote cultural values and distinctiveness.

---

[24] "Taxing the WTO to the Limit," Financial Times, September 4, 2000, p. 8.

These disputes tend to involve complex new issues that have arisen as a result of increased economic interdependence and of significant U.S.-EU differences in regulatory approaches. The EU approach to regulation is based on the notion that every important economic activity should take place under a legal framework, whereas the central premise of the U.S. approach is that government does not need to regulate unless a problem arises.

While the impact on trade may be the same as in other disputes, these conflicts are often characterized by delicate considerations of motives. Parties that have initiated the action, often consumer or environmental groups, tend to view the protective impact as an indirect consequence of an attempt to attain some valid domestic objective. Trade barriers motivated by food safety, for example, may be considered more legitimate by the public than barriers motivated by economic protectionism. If food safety is perceived as being sacrificed to free trade, support for free trade would erode. Similarly, if food safety is used as a disguise for protectionism, support for free trade could also erode.

The four disputes summarized below are rooted in different regulatory approaches and public preferences. Disputes over beef hormones and genetically engineered crops stem primarily from stronger European societal preferences for high food safety standards. A longstanding dispute over the EU's audio-visual sector has a strong cultural basis, steeped in a perceived need to preserve West European society from U.S. dominance. And a clash over an EU regulation banning airplanes outfitted with "hushkitted" or retooled engines ostensibly was driven by environmental demands to reduce noise pollution surrounding European airports.

Numerous other disputes could also be included in the following discussion. For example, a dispute over data privacy reflects very different approaches between the U.S. and EU, as well as popular attitudes, towards the protection of personal information that is transmitted electronically. The issue of "multi-functionality" in agriculture, where the Europeans claim agriculture is more than just another industry, has deep cultural roots that divide the two sides. Disputes involving environmental, wildlife, and animal welfare protection, such as U.S. restrictions on imports of tuna from Europe and EU efforts to ban fur imports from the United States, also reflect competing social and cultural differences.

Beef Hormones. The dispute over the EU ban, implemented in 1989, on the production and importation of meat treated with growth-promoting hormones has been one of the most bitter and intractable trade disputes between the United States and Europe. It is also a dispute that, on its surface, involves a relatively small amount of trade. The ban affected an estimated $100-$200 million in lost U.S. exports — less than one-tenth of one percent of U.S. exports to the EU in 1999. But the dispute has played off each side's sovereign right to regulate the safety of its food against its WTO obligations.[25]

The EU justified the ban to protect the health and safety of consumers, but several WTO dispute settlement panels subsequently ruled that the ban was inconsistent with the Uruguay Round Sanitary and Phytosanitary (SPS) Agreement. The SPS Agreement provides criteria that have to be met when a country imposes food safety import regulations more stringent than those agreed upon in international standards. These include a scientific assessment that the hormones pose a health risk, along with a risk assessment. Although the WTO panels concluded that the EU ban lacked a scientific justification, the EU refused to remove the ban primarily out of concern that European consumers were opposed to having this kind of meat in the marketplace.

In lieu of lifting the ban, the EU in 1999 offered the United States compensation in the form of an expanded quota for hormone-free beef. The U.S. government, backed by most of the U.S. beef industry, opposed compensation on the grounds that exports of hormone-free meat would not be large enough to compensate for losses of hormone-treated exports. This led the way for the United States to impose 100% retaliatory tariffs on $116 million of EU agricultural products from mostly France, Germany, Italy, and Denmark, countries deemed the biggest supporters of the ban. These tariffs, in turn, sparked protests among French and European farmers, who seized on the beef hormones case as a symbol of the threat pose by Americanization and globalization to European regulations and traditions.[26]

The U.S. hard line was buttressed by concerns that other countries might adopt similar measures based on health concerns that lack an objective scientific basis according to U.S. standards. Other U.S. interest groups are concerned that noncompliance by the EU undermines the future ability of the WTO to resolve disputes involving the use of SPS measures.

In October 2003, the European Commission notified the WTO that it had changed its hormone ban legislation in a way that it believes complies with international trade rules. The legislation made provisional a previous permanent ban for five growth hormones used to raise beef and keeps in place a permanent ban on the use of oestradiaol 17 on the basis that it is a carcinogen. As a result,

---

[25] Pollack, Mark A. "Political Economy of Transatlantic Trade Disputes," in *Transatlantic Economic Disputes*, p. 75.

the EU argued that it should no longer be subject to punitive trade sanctions by the United States (as well as by Canada), and on November 8, 2004, took the initial step in the WTO to challenge the U.S. and Canadian sanctions still in effect. The U.S. and meat industry, however, argued that making a ban provisional for the long term does not meet WTO obligations. Nevertheless, in February 2005, the EU secured the establishment of a panel to determine whether the United States and Canada were in violation of WTO rules by maintaining punitive tariffs on a number of EU products in the dispute. A WTO dispute panel hearing on this issue was held on August 1, 2005. A second hearing was scheduled for November 2005 but later was postponed to September 2006. Agreement on the selection of scientific experts has been elusive, making process of settling the dispute even more difficult. Thus, so long as th EU refuses to eliminate or modify the ban, U.S. retaliatory tariffs are likely to remain in effect.

Genetically Engineered Crops.[27] Differences between the United States and the EU over genetically engineered (GE) crops and food products that contain them pose a potential threat to, and in some cases have already disrupted, U.S. agricultural trade. Underlying the conflicts are pronounced differences between the United States and EU about GE products and their potential health and environmental effects.

Widespread farmer adoption of bio-engineered crops in the United States makes consumer acceptance of GE crops and foods at home and abroad critical to producers, processors, and exporters. U.S. farmers use GE crops because they can reduce input costs or make field work more flexible. Supporters of GE crops maintain that the technology also holds promise for enhancing agricultural productivity and improving nutrition in developing countries. U.S. consumers, with some exceptions, have been generally accepting of the health and safety of GE foods and willing to put their trust in a credible regulatory process.

In contrast, EU consumers, environmentalists, and some scientists maintain that the long-term effects of GE foods on health and the environment are unknown and not scientifically established. By and large, Europeans are more risk averse to the human health and safety issues associated with bio-engineered food products than U.S. citizens.

---

[26] Pollack, Mark A. "Political Economy of Transatlantic Trade Dispute," in *Transatlantic Economic Disputes,* p. 76.

[27] Prepared by Charles Hanrahan, Specialist in Agriculture, Resources, Science, and Industry. For further discussion, see CRS Report RS2 1556, *Agricultural Biotechnology: The U.S. - EU Dispute.*

In 1999 the EU instituted a *de facto* moratorium on any new approval of GE products. The moratorium halted some $300 million in annual U.S. corn shipments. EU policymakers also moved toward establishing mandatory labeling requirements for products containing GE ingredients.

For several years, U.S. trade officials refrained from challenging the EU moratorium in the WTO, partly out of fear that the EU, if it lost the case, would not comply due to public opposition. But in May 2003, facing the potential spread of the EU approach to third countries, the United States (along with Canada, and Argentina) challenged the EU de facto moratorium in the WTO.

Although the EU effectively lifted the moratorium in May 2004 by approving a genetically engineered corn variety, the three complainants pursued the case, in part because a number of EU member states continued to block approved biotech products. On February 7, 2006, the WTO, in an interim confidential report, ruled that a moratorium had existed, that bans on EU-approved genetically-engineered crops in six EU member countries violated WTO rules, and that the EU failed to ensure that its approval procedures were conducted without "undue delay." Some other claims by the United States were rejected. With the legal battle likely to continue for several years, this dispute still has considerable potential to adversely affect transatlantic relations.

Audio-Visual Sector. This dispute dates back to 1989 when the EU issued a Broadcast Directive that required that a majority of entertainment broadcast transmission time be reserved for programs of European origin "where practicable" and "by appropriate means." All EU member states, including the ten new Member States, have enacted legislation implementing the Broadcast Directive.[28]

Implementation of the directive has varied from country to country. In general, efforts to strengthen European content quotas have failed to materialize, but a number of countries have passed specific laws that hinder the free flow of programming. France, for example, has prime time rules that limit the access of U.S.

programs in prime time. Radio broadcast quotas also limit broadcasts of American music. Italy also has a European content prime time rule, as well as requirements that large movie theaters show EU films on a "stable" basis.

Within the EU, the Broadcast Directive has been controversial. Efforts to tighten restrictions have been opposed by Germany and Britain and by some elements of the European industry. Moreover, consumer demand for foreign

---

[28] Office of the United States Trade Representative, *2005 Trade Barrier Report*, p. 264.

movies, coupled with technological innovation through the introduction of cable and satellite television, have undermined movement in the direction of increased protection.

The dispute highlights European concerns, particularly in France and Italy, about creeping "Americanization" threatening to undermine their national identities and cultures. It also underlines a fundamental U.S.-EU divide over the role of cultural and social issues in trade disputes. While the U.S. tends to assign priority weight to maximizing the economic value of efficiency in trade negotiations, the EU, by attitude and law, places more weight on environmental and cultural values.

Aircraft Hushkits. European skies are quite crowded with aircraft, airports tend to be situated in heavily populated areas, and there is a serious noise problem. Public concerns about aircraft noise are combined with environmental policy discussions about emissions and greenhouse gases. To deal with this problem, the EU attempted in 1997 to develop an EU-wide noise standard. When it became clear that any such standard would likely impose high economic costs on European manufactures and airlines, the EU advanced a regulation that would limit the operation of "hushkitted" aircraft in European skies.

Hushkitting is a process that involves a combination of strategies, including renovated engine enclosures and replacement engine components, designed to reduce aircraft noise. Under standards adopted by the EU, it did not provide major reductions in noise levels.[29]

As formally implemented by the EU on May 4, 2000, the vast majority of aircraft affected by the regulation were of U.S. manufacture. Also adversely affected were mostly U.S. manufacturers of noise reduction technology and new engines for older aircraft. Conversely, all European Airbus aircraft are unaffected and there were no major European hushkit producers. The U.S. aerospace industry estimated that the regulation has cost its airlines and manufacturers $2 billion.

On March 14, 2000, the United States filed a motion with the International Civil Aviation Organization (ICAO) seeking relief from the EU's regulation. The U.S. case maintained that the regulation did not comply with ICAO regulations and discriminated against U.S. interests. Proceedings were suspended pending

---

[29] For a full discussion, see CRS Report RL30547, *Aircraft Hushkits: Noise and International Trade*, by John W. Fischer.

settlement negotiations. In early 2002, a settlement was reached under which the EU repealed the regulation and the U.S. withdrew its complaint.[30]

CONFLICT MANAGEMENT

The three categories of trade conflicts — traditional, foreign policy, and regulatory — appear to offer different possibilities for conflict management. This is due not only to the fact that the causes and dimensions of these categories of conflicts differ, but also because the institutional relationships and forces that affect the supply of and demand for protection are operative in varying degrees from category to category. These factors include the presence or absence of bilateral or multilateral agreements and rules that govern the settlement of the disputes, the extent to which the disputes fit into the standard free trade versus protectionism dichotomy, the relevance of underlying economic and political trends, and the effectiveness of other institutional arrangements designed to prevent or resolve the disputes.

- Bilateral and multilateral trade agreements can dampen the inclination of governments to supply protection and the private sector to demand protection by providing a fairly detailed "road map" of permissible actions and obligations. While often litigated and disputed, the obligations tend to be relatively clear-cut and help resolve disagreements. When new spats arise, built-in procedures of many agreements can facilitate a settlement or help avoid escalation.

- Conflicts that fall into the standard free trade versus protectionism dichotomy also have a built-in potential for undercutting any rationale governments may have to supply protection or private parties may use in demanding protection. This happens due to an ideological consensus in both the U.S. and EU in favor of resisting protectionism on both economic and political grounds. As a result, most demands for protection from producer interests must be justified as exceptions to the generalized support for freer trade arrangements and policies.

---

[30] Abbott, Kenneth W. "U.S.-EU Disputes Over Technical Barriers to Trade and the 'Hushkit' Dispute, In *Transatlantic Economic Disputes,* pp. 247-280.

- Diverse economic and political trends can also suppress the supply and demand for protection. For example, declining support for industrial policy initiatives, as has been the case in both the U.S. and EU, could make industry-specific pleas for government assistance less compelling. High priority political commitments, such as the EU's policy towards enlargement, may also create incentives for reform and liberalization as opposed to protection.

- Both formal and informal cooperative arrangements have proliferated over the past decade to better manage transatlantic trade disputes. These have included efforts to strengthen regulatory cooperation and the establishment of forums for bilateral consultations. By attempting to incorporate the views of a wider range of domestic interest groups, these efforts have also aimed at preventing disputes from arising.

Applying these factors to the three categories of trade disputes, there are grounds for judging that traditional trade conflicts may become less disruptive to the bilateral relationship in the future, but more limited grounds for projecting a diminution of foreign policy induced friction. The prospects for future domestic-policy related trade disputes fall somewhere in between these two extremes, with reasons for foreseeing a reduction in friction associated with some disputes, but not all. The basis for this assessment is presented below.

TRADITIONAL TRADE CONFLICT

Traditional trade conflicts, involving demands from producer interests for protection or state aids, by definition raise fairly routine commercial questions that have been addressed by governments for decades. As a result, most are governed by some bilateral or multilateral agreement or understanding. The WTO in particular provides a body of multilateral rules governing the use of tariffs and other restrictive trade practices and a forum for consultation and dispute resolution. And in the event of non-compliance with WTO rulings, retaliation can be authorized to provide incentives for compliance with WTO rulings. Disputes involving agriculture, aerospace, steel, and contingency protection have all been tempered by the WTO framework of rules and obligations.

The Uruguay Round Agreement on Agriculture significantly dampened trade conflict in the areas of EU home market protection and export subsidy wars for third country markets. The multilateral agreement on subsidies provides the terms of engagement for the current clashes over "launch" aid for the A380. Steel trade conflict in recent years has pivoted around the utilization of anti-dumping and safeguard laws, procedures that both the U.S. and EU employ with considerable frequency and which both sides in the past have considered legitimate. The fact that the steel trade battle in 2002 was so heated may stem from a mutual perception that each side did not adhere to the letter or spirit of the safeguards agreement.

Traditional trade conflicts also tend to fit into the standard free trade versus protectionism dichotomy. As in the case of agriculture, aerospace, steel, and the Byrd Amendment, proposals or requests for additional protection or promotion will be subject to full transparency, investigation, and debate. Given that both the United States and European Union have open societies with an ideological consensus in favor of competition and open markets, petitioners for protection will have the burden of arguing that their request merits being excepted from the dominant policy orientation.

Several economic and political trends may also serve to limit future disputes involving producer protection. These include a decline of support for industrial policy in both Brussels and Washington, budgetary pressures in the EU, and a rising level of foreign direct investment and corporate mergers.

industries, were considerable in the late 1 980s and early 1990s in both the EU and United States. Based on new rationales for targeted assistance from states, the support for industrial policies posed new challenges to the maintenance of free trade orthodoxy. For a variety of reasons, such policies today are viewed more skeptically in both Brussels and Washington, thereby lessening pressures for what many observers construed as a new and disguised vehicle for protectionism.

The issue of subsidies or state aids is closely related to the industrial policy debate. In Europe, with the movement towards a single market that is deregulated and more competitive, subsidies and state aids to individual companies have been increasingly challenged, scrutinized, and curtailed. This trend, which is reenforced by budgetary constraints associated with fiscal targets required of member states participating in the European Monetary

Union, could serve not only as a strong force for reducing conflict in aviation and steel, but in other sectors as well.[31]

A rising level of foreign direct investment and a wave of new corporate mergers are also forces for dampening demands for protection. As these trends accelerate, many formerly domestic or nationally-based industries will become increasingly globalized. As transatlantic merger and acquisition activity picks up, the answer to the question of 'who is us?' becomes increasingly blurred. Even in the production of a new Airbus plane, it is estimated that American suppliers will provide a considerable amount of the sourcing of the parts. These developments, in turn, tend to create forces that may moderate demands for protection.[32]

A number of cross currents, of course, could create a much different outlook. Historically, many industries have been quite creative and successful in justifying demands for protection based on some unique argument. This has been particularly true in the area of agriculture where both sides have argued that agriculture is not just another industry. The strength of the European agricultural lobby rests in part on public support for it as a means of preserving a way of life and a particular kind of environment perceived as worth preserving. On-going efforts in Brussels to reform the CAP must deal with this challenge.

Morever, fundamental economic conditions can change rapidly. Bumper world crops creating an oversupply of basic agricultural commodities or an economic downturn creating an over-supply of steel could ignite old trade battles in steel and agriculture once again.

FOREIGN POLICY CONFLICT

Unlike traditional trade conflicts, foreign policy inspired trade squabbles tend to lack the same kind of institutional arrangements and pressures that dampen the supply of and demand for protection. Nor are these conflicts easily framed along free trade and protectionism lines. Some of these conflicts, but not all, may be moderated in the future by lobbying efforts of big business on both sides of the Atlantic to maintain stable commercial ties. However, if Brussels or Washington is determined to use trade to achieve foreign policy

[31] Kahler, Miles. *Regional Futures and Transatlantic Economic Relations,* European Studies Association, 1995, p. 50.

[32] Kahler, Miles. *Regional Futures and Transatlantic Economic Relations,* European Studies Association, 1995, p. 51.

objectives, lobbying efforts are unlikely to be successful in the absence of a transatlantic agreement to treat these issues in a more consistent fashion.

In most U.S. -EU sanctions conflicts, there are no bilateral or multilateral understandings that can help resolve very basic foreign policy differences over how to respond to violations by third countries of international norms affecting human rights or security. Many trade measures taken in a foreign policy context are either exempt from WTO disciplines because they are either mandated by the United Nations or applied against non-WTO countries, or only very loosely regulated by the WTO. The latter arises because the national security provision of GATT (Article 21) provides wide latitude for countries to pursue sanctions if they deem the measures to be in their national security interest.[33]

WTO rules also provide little guidance and "rules of the road" concerning preferential regional agreements. While the WTO set up a new Committee on Regional Trade Agreements in 1995 to highlight abuses of Article 24 provisions that allow regional agreements to deviate from the non-discrimination principle of the WTO, few challenges have been launched. A major obstacle has been the difficulty of measuring the value of trade diverted from efficient producers to the beneficiaries of preferences granted. As a result, the drive to cut preferential deals continues to grow (along with mistrust) while the ability to challenge deals that raise new trade barriers remains quite weak. As the U.S. and EU embark on even more aggressive efforts to negotiate preferential trade agreements, increased conflict in this area may develop.[34]

While the U.S. pursuit of market opening through unilateral means has declined since passage of the Uruguay Round Agreements in 1995, pressures in the United States to revisit this issue could grow. The EU's refusal to implement WTO panel findings on bananas and beef hormones, coupled with continued attacks on U.S. trade laws, could lead U.S. policymakers to reconsider this Uruguay Round bargain of limits imposed on unilateralism in return for a more binding dispute settlement process.

The dispute over the U.S. export tax benefit program raises a different issue. It can be argued that the WTO was not the proper forum in which the dispute should have been pursued. But existing WTO "rules of the road" evidently presented a target of opportunity for achieving other foreign policy goals, namely enhancing the EU's negotiating leverage vis-à-vis Washington.

---

[33] Schott, Jeffrey, "Whither U.S.- European Trade Relations?," p. 59.

Pressures and temptations to apply sanctions against countries that violate international norms, to cut preferential trade deals, to act unilaterally in the pursuit of national trade interests, and to use the WTO to achieve foreign policy objectives are unlikely to go away. Nor are efforts of big and pro-trade business lobbies to curb future actions along these lines likely to be successful in the absence of a broad diplomatic undertaking or a pledge committing both sides to refrain from such actions. Such a pledge or non-aggression pact has been suggested as a way to bring greater coherence in areas of disagreement and in helping to achieve shared goals in a less contentious atmosphere. But little progress has been made, perhaps due to the high level of mutual suspicions, differences in diplomatic approaches, and foreign policy-making machinery.[35]

REGULATORY POLICY CONFLICT

U.S.-EU trade disputes have focused increasingly on differences in regulation, rather than traditional barriers such as tariffs or subsidies. Regulatory requirements established primarily with legitimate domestic concerns of consumer and environmental protection or public health in mind do not discriminate (at least directly) between domestic and imported goods and services. But they may have the secondary effect of distorting or discriminating against the free flow of international trade, which in turn leads to disputes. For this reason, transatlantic regulatory disputes can be more bitter and difficult to resolve than traditional trade disputes, in so far as both sides feel their actions are justified by democratically derived decisions. In this context, such disputes are often difficult to resolve within the context of the WTO because they require a balancing of domestic concerns with international obligations.[36]

In trying to resolve or prevent most regulatory disputes, the United States and the EU have tended to rely more on bilateral cooperation and negotiation than on the WTO dispute resolution system. The two sides have

---

[34] See CRS Report RL3 3463, *Trade Negotiations in the 110th Congress*, by Ian F. Fergusson, and CRS Report RS22547, *Europe's New Trade Agenda*, by Raymond J. Ahearn.

[35] Frost, Ellen L. *Transatlantic Trade: A Strategic Agenda*. Institute for International Economics, 1997, pp. 54-64.

[36] Mark A. Pollack, "Political Economy of Transatlantic Trade Disputes," in *Transatlantic Economic Disputes*, p. 71.

made much progress bilaterally in mitigating divergent standards and certification systems as a source of bilateral trade conflict.

Bilateral efforts to promote regulatory cooperation have been a top priority in both governments and private sectors since the signing of the "New Transatlantic Agenda" (NTA) and "Action Plan" in late 1995. The creation of the Transatlantic Business Dialogue (TABD), a multinational corporation-led initiative to lower trade and investment barriers across the Atlantic, spearheaded efforts to focus particular attention on problems posed by divergent standards and certification systems. In addition to promoting convergence in regulatory systems through the principle of "approved once, accepted everywhere," efforts were undertaken to negotiate mutual recognition agreements (MRAs) covering key sectors such as pharmaceuticals and medical devices, and telecommunications equipment.[37]

In June 1997, the two sides reached agreement on a package of MRA's affecting six sectors, including electrical equipment, pharmaceutical products, telecommunications and information technology equipment. Each side basically accepted the others' inspection, testing, and certification standards in these sectors. The agreements, which covered around $50 billion in U.S.-EU trade, allowed European companies to sell products directly into the U.S. market after they have been tested and certified to U.S. health and safety standards, and vice versa.[38]

Under the 1998 Transatlantic Economic Partnership (TEP), the two sides agreed to begin negotiation of MRA's in other sectors, including regulatory processes connected with biotechnology. But negotiating and implementing these agreements have proven difficult due to very different industry interests and regulatory approaches of the United States and the EU.[39]

More recently, German Chancellor Angela Merkel in January 2007 proposed the creation of a Transatlantic Free Trade Area (TAFTA). With Germany having assumed the Presidency of the EU for the first six months of 2007, Merkel's initiative aims to harmonize regulations across the Atlantic and reduce non-tariff barriers that constrain the free flow of capital, goods, and services.

There are numerous challenges raised by the application of modern biotechnology to food production. The Uruguay Round Sanitary and Phytosanitary Standards (SPS) Agreement was designed to deal with

---

[37] Schott, Jeffrey. "Whither U.S. -European Trade Relations," p. 56.

[38] Frost, Ellen. *Transatlantic Trade: A Strategic Agenda,* p. 6.

[39] Mark A. Pollack, "Political Economy of Transatlantic Trade Disputes," in *Transatlantic Economic Disputes*, p. 98.

this issue. It requires countries that impose regulations or trade bans to protect the health of plants, animals, and people to base such decisions on risk assessments on sound scientific evidence.[40] But the SPS requirement of a sound scientific basis is open to varying interpretations.

Ambiguities in the SPS agreement are complicated because many European consumers may believe that avoidance of production practices associated with biotechnology is a value in itself. For these consumers, scientific studies showing that such technologies do not result in threats to human or animal health may not be convincing. Given these strong views, many European officials want leeway to impose trade restrictions on a "precautionary basis" and others want to renegotiate the SPS agreement. Both avenues could open up a large loophole for discriminatory trade barriers.

More ominously, some analysts are concerned that European agricultural policy makers may be "under pressures to guarantee higher levels of safety than strictly is necessary in order to maintain consumer confidence in the food system."[41] Even if these conflicts are not primarily due to the deliberate use of health, safety, or environmental standards as trade barriers, mistrust grows in terms of how much effort government authorities may have put into managing public concerns through educational efforts. Under these circumstances, one analyst has argued that trade disputes resulting from such differences are unlikely ever to be resolved; at best they can be contained.[42]

On the other hand, transatlantic consumer views may be converging in some areas. For example, while U.S. consumers generally have been quite receptive to genetically modified organisms (GMOs), Kraft Foods' nationwide recall in 2000 of taco shells that contained a genetically engineered corn not approved for human consumption indicates some underlying discontent. The recall was initiated by a coalition of environmental and consumer groups critical of bio-engineered food.[43] Others argue that in a number of other areas, including corporate mergers and Internet privacy, the European Union's more active role in protecting consumers will gain

---

[40] A related multilateral code, the Agreement on Technical Barriers to Trade (TBT), covers other types of regulations such as labeling and packaging.

[41] Josling, Tim. "Comment on Stefan Tangermann," in *Transatlantic Relations in a Global Economy*, p.166

[42] Vogel, David. *Barriers or Benefits?*, Brookings Institution, 1997. p. 62.

[43] Pollack, Andrew. "Kraft Recalls Taco Shells With Bio-engineered Corn," *Washington Post*, September 23, 2000, p. B1.

growing appreciation and support in the United States.[44] At the same time, the European Commission is seeking actively to recreate an approval process for GMO crops, moving to establish a pan-EU food agency, and proposing action to provide consumers with more information on GM foods.

In other disputes, technological progress can be a force for change. The audio-visual dispute is a case in point where EU efforts to increase protection of this sector have faced growing technological obstacles, as well as consumer resistance. Rapid technological innovation in the form of cable and satellite television, innovations strongly supported by consumers, offer new products that are difficult to block or regulate. Regulations in this environment often are too complex to enforce or, if enforced, prove adverse to the interests of European producers.[45]

TRADE CONFLICT IN PERSPECTIVE

Mark Twain reportedly once said of Wagner's music that "it is not as bad as it sounds." Similarly, U.S.-EU trade conflicts may not be as ominous and threatening as they appear. Despite the rise in trade tensions and episodes of tit-for-tat retaliation over the past few years, the notion that the relationship between the world's two most powerful economic powers is constantly teetering on the brink of a transatlantic trade war seems a stretch. Nor does it appear that the trade conflicts represent or symbolize any kind of fundamental rift that is possibly developing between the United States and Europe.

At the same time, the disputes do not appear to be ephemeral distractions or mere consequences of a mass media that tends to sensationalize and define the relationship unfairly. Nor are they products of trade negotiators, who like generals, are often accused of fighting the last war. Nor are they trivial or silly squabbles because they represent a mere 1-2% of transatlantic trade.

Trade conflicts rather appear to have real, albeit limited, economic and political consequences for the bilateral relationship. Perhaps more significantly, trade disputes may also pose very real obstacles for the two partners in their efforts to play a leadership role in promoting a more open and prosperous world economy.

---

[44] Richter, Stephan-Gotz, "The U.S. Consumer's Friend," *New York Times,* September 21, 2000, p. A31.
[45] Kahler, Miles. *Regional Futures and Transatlantic Economic Relations,* Brookings Institution, 1997, p. 53.

This is particularly evident in the way bilateral trade disputes may be testing the functioning of the World Trade Organization.

Relationship Impact

The economic and political impacts that result from U. S.-EU trade disputes can be easily identified, but are much harder to quantify. In both cases, a variety of forces effectively contains the economic and political costs from rising or getting out of hand.

The $300 million in retaliatory U.S. tariffs levied on European exports over the banana and beef disputes and the over $2 billion in EU tariffs imposed on U.S. exports over the FSC (now suspended) and Byrd Amendment disputes provide the most visible economic costs of trade conflict. The retaliatory tariffs are designed to dramatically increase the costs of selective European and U.S. products, making it much more difficult for those "targeted" foreign producers to sell in the U.S. or EU markets. In theory, foreign exporters denied access to markets are expected to pressure their respective governments to change the policies that are in violation of WTO rules.

Retaliation is not, however, cost-free. The process also hurts importers, consumers, and firms dependent on those imports as inputs in their production process. These entities intensively lobby Congress and the European Commission to keep their products off any retaliation list that is drawn up. Domestic political pressures, thus, limit the scope and flexibility trade officials on both sides of the Atlantic have in devising a retaliation list. As a result, most retaliation lists tend to be dominated by luxury items or high value-added agricultural items that are produced by both economic superpowers. Under these conditions, coming up with a list of products whose export value matches the relatively small sum of a few billion dollars is no easy task.[46]

Attempts by either Brussels or Washington to retaliate on a much larger value of trade could be expected to ignite a firestorm of political opposition. The huge stake each side has in the other's market through foreign direct investments, merger and acquisition activity, combined with "globalized" patterns of production, would likely serve as major counter-forces to any rise in

---

[46] The task is further complicated by the incomes and tastes of American consumers. The 100% tariffs levied against European products such as truffles, jams, Roquefort cheese, chicory, specialized mustard, and biscuits have had very little impact in cutting back on sales in the United States over the past year. "Administration Still Uncertain on Carousel," *Washington Trade Daily,* September 26, 2000.

trade warfare. These trends create extensive overlapping interests among companies and strong incentives to contain disputes. In globally traded sectors, mass production in a single location is becoming rare as companies source inputs, research, design, and marketing strategies from all over the world. This, in turn, shrinks the scope of, as well as complicates, the definition of what is domestic production or a domestic company.

In terms of political impacts, trade disputes likely have some effect on public opinion and attitudes, as well as connect in some way to other transatlantic problems. Polls indicate that there is a great deal of fear in Europe that the United States, due to the strength of its economy, has the ability to impose both economic and social changes on the rest of the world. This fear and perhaps frustration may translate into antipathy to the United States, often expressed as anti-Americanism. U.S. retaliation against Europe for not accepting hormone-enhanced beef, for example, may only fuel these generalized anti-American feelings that the United States is a bully.[47]

The reaction to U.S. retaliation may be even more acute among some European policymakers. By selectively targeting only those EU members that have clearly benefitted from WTO illegal policies, many European policymakers view retaliation as a frontal assault on European unity — an old-fashioned divide-and-conquer strategy.[48] Commenting on the U.S. proposal to rotate items under trade sanctions from product to product and country to country, French President Chirac complained bitterly that carousel retaliation is "much closer to 1 9th Century gunboat diplomacy than to 21st Century diplomacy."[49]

Whether or how these reactions affect cooperation in other problem areas is difficult to know. Clearly, if trade tensions work to undermine the notion that the United States and Europe share common interests or lead to a view that a weaker Europe or a weaker America is in the other's interest, then the consequences could be major. But there is no evidence to suggest that this is happening as the United States and the EU to date have been able to compartmentalize trade problems to a remarkable degree.

---

[47] Daly, Suzanne. "More Vehemently Than Ever, Europe Is Scorning the United States," *New York Times,* April 9, 2000, p. 1.

[48] Ironically, some observers see trade disputes as an instrument for promoting EU unity. This view is that trade conflict with the U.S. may provide EU policymakers with a convenient "enemy" that can help divert attention from internal problems and disagreements. While this may be true for some disputes where there is a unified EU view, on most trade disputes there are often different views and positions among the member states.

[49] Trade Reports International Group, *Washington Trade Daily,* September 8, 2000.

LEADERSHIP IMPACT

Trade disputes may have discernible impacts on U.S.-EU efforts to provide leadership of the world economy. The disputes absorb a significant amount of time and energy of key policymakers at the expense of efforts to pursue common interests and objectives, such as completing the Doha round of multilateral trade negotiations. Moreover, the two powers need to set an example of cooperation and adherence to WTO rules if the whole system is not to unravel.

The credibility of the WTO depends critically on a prompt, effective, and fair dispute-settlement mechanism. Unfortunately, the EU is seen by U.S. policymakers and interest groups affected by the beef and banana cases as having used every loophole to delay decisions and then refuse to comply with panel decisions. Similarly, U.S. compliance efforts in FSC and Byrd Amendment disputes are found wanting by EU policymakers. While only a handful of U. S.-EU WTO disputes have ended in withdrawal of concessions (i.e. retaliation) since 1995, non-compliance by a key member arguably weakens the authority of the WTO and serves as a poor model for the rest of the world.[50] Why should we comply with WTO panel decisions if the EU does not have to, many countries ask. Non-compliance by one of the two leading economic powers is also said to diminish the perceived value of negotiating new trade agreements.[51]

Both the U.S. and EU (bananas in the case of the U.S. and the FSC in the case of the EU) have brought complaints to the WTO that may have been motivated more by a desire to score points with domestic political interests or to rack up negotiating leverage by successfully prosecuting cases than to address serious trade problems. To the extent that a charge of capricious use of the dispute settlement process is valid, the WTO as an institution may also be weakened. Some may argue that no institution can survive for long this kind of treatment by the body's two biggest members.

To deal with the problem of non-compliance, the U.S. and EU have legalistic and diplomatic options. In the area of some of the most bitter U.S.-EU disagreements, particularly over GMOs, the WTO may be asked to make decisions on very complex issues that go deep into the domestic social and the environmental life of each side. Binding rulings in areas that have strong domestic roots can raise sovereignty issues and court a public backlash. Under these circumstances, where the formulations of right and wrong are

---

[50] "Transatlantic Trade Tensions," *Financial Times,* May 17, 2000, p. 8.

[51] Schott, Jeffrey. "After Seattle," *The Economist,* August 26, 2000, p. 66.

increasingly blurred, it may be legitimate to question whether WTO panels should be asked to clarify vague rules where there is little U.S.-EU consensus, or whether trade officials should attempt to negotiate diplomatic solutions to disagreements that are so difficult to resolve.

CHAPTER SOURCES

The following chapters have been previously published:

Chapter 1 – This is an edited, excerpted and augmented edition of a United States Congressional Research Service publication, Report Order Code RS21556, dated January 28, 2009.

Chapter 2 – This is an edited, excerpted and augmented edition of a United States Congressional Research Service publication, Report Order Code RS21372, dated July 3, 2008.

Chapter 3 – This is an edited, excerpted and augmented edition of a United States Congressional Research Service publication, Report Order Code RL34381, dated April 8, 2008.

Chapter 4 – This is an edited, excerpted and augmented edition of a United States Congressional Research Service publication, Report Order Code RS22547, dated July 31, 2008.

Chapter 5 – This is an edited, excerpted and augmented edition of a United States Congressional Research Service publication, Report Order Code RL30608, dated January 28, 2009.

Chapter 6 – This is an edited, excerpted and augmented edition of a United States Congressional Research Service publication, Report Order Code RL30732, dated April 11, 2007.

INDEX

A

academics, 23, 88
accounting, x, 34, 39, 42, 71, 79
accounting standards, 42
adjustment, 100
aerospace, viii, xii, 21, 23, 31, 83, 91, 94, 107, 109, 110
Africa, 16, 17, 88, 100
agricultural exports, vii, 1, 34, 36
agricultural sector, 91, 93
agriculture, xii, 12, 13, 27, 38, 67, 80, 83, 88, 89, 91, 92, 93, 103, 109, 110, 111
Air Force, 33, 59, 96
airports, 31, 40, 94, 103, 107
antidumping, 75, 96, 97, 100
antitrust, viii, 22, 23, 47, 48, 49, 50, 52, 53, 54, 60, 62
Argentina, vii, 1, 3, 7, 36, 64, 106
ASEAN, 64, 69
Asia, 47, 70, 101
assessment, 2, 35, 37, 104, 109
assets, 16, 17, 25, 78
attitudes, 7, 9, 34, 36, 103, 118
Attorney General, 60, 61
Austria, 2, 11, 14, 19, 37, 58, 80
authority, 5, 119
avoidance, 56, 115

B

background, ix, xi, 22, 23, 58, 73
background information, ix, xi, 22, 23, 58, 73
balance of payments, 77, 81
Balkans, 15, 17
banking, 39, 45, 79
banks, 43, 45
barriers, ix, x, xii, 22, 23, 26, 27, 28, 29, 30, 40, 47, 55, 56, 67, 72, 79, 83, 89, 91, 92, 100, 103, 112, 113, 114, 115
beef, viii, xii, 7, 18, 21, 23, 35, 56, 57, 67, 80, 84, 92, 93, 101, 103, 104, 112, 117, 118, 119
behavior, 48, 51, 52
Belgium, 7, 11, 14, 58, 80
binding, 12, 13, 28, 112
biotechnology, vii, 1, 3, 4, 5, 8, 36, 37, 56, 91, 114, 115
bonds, 25, 32, 79, 85
Brazil, 7, 55, 64
breakdown, ix, 63
Britain, 16, 106
Bulgaria, 11, 14, 58, 80, 85
Burma, 99

M

N

O